The War in Italy

The War in Italy
The Second Italian War
of Independence, 1859

With 40 Duotone Illustrations by
Carlo Bossoli
and 2 maps

Text by
John E. Tuel

LEONAUR

The War in Italy: The Second Italian War of Independence, 1859
Text by John E. Tuel
Illustrations by Carlo Bossoli

Leonaur is an imprint of Oakpast Ltd

ISBN: 978-0-85706-000-0 (hardcover)
ISBN: 978-0-85706-000-0 (softcover)

http://www.leonaur.com

Publisher's Notes

The views expressed in this book are not necessarily
those of the publisher.

Contents

Preface

This work being, as its title indicates, a descriptive narrative of the war in Italy, politics do not come within its sphere. The reader will find the account, in its main features, corresponding with the letters which were written by the author from the allied camp, and which appeared in *The Times*. Whatever variations he may find between the latter and the present narrative, are explained by the difference which must always exist between letters written on the spot, under the first impression of the moment, and a connected account written several months later, when many new details have become known, when much that was doubtful could be cleared up, and when many erroneous impressions could be corrected.

With all this, the work does not pretend to minute accuracy; three months after the events this would be presumption. It is a carefully-drawn picture of the campaign as it presents itself to the mind of the author now, when he has had opportunity to revisit the principal scenes of action and to control his own impressions by the official accounts on both sides, and by the abundant materials which have been accessible to him since the end of the war.

The Author
Milan,
November 3, 1859

CHAPTER 1

Declaration of War

On the 19th of April Count Buol addressed to Count Cavour his ultimatum, by which he demanded, in the name of the Austrian government, the disarming of Sardinia and the disbanding of the Italian volunteers, fixing a period of three days for an answer to this demand. This ultimatum, tantamount to a declaration of war, was presented at Turin by Baron de Kellersberg on the 23rd of April, at half-past five p.m.; and on the 26th, at half-past six p.m., the Austrian envoy, having received a negative answer, left the Sardinian capital with Colonel Govoin, of the Piedmontese staff, who accompanied him to the frontier.

Even before the Austrian ultimatum was presented at Turin, Europe could not doubt that war was impending. Two days before, Paris and Lyons had been in a state of excitement, the troops of the garrison having received orders to start for Toulon and Grenoble; and the next day, the 22nd, the *Moniteur* informed France officially that Austria, refusing to consent to a general disarmament proposed by England, had addressed an ultimatum to the Sardinian government, summoning it to disarm within three days; and that in consequence of these facts the emperor had ordered the concentration of several divisions on the frontiers of Piedmont. The same day a royal ordinance appeared at Turin dividing the Sardinian army into five divisions of infantry and one of cavalry, and placing the first division under the command of General Durando, the second under Fanti, the third under Castelborgo, the fourth under Cialdini, the fifth under Cucchiari, and the cavalry under General Sonnaz; the king reserving to himself the command in chief, with General La Marmora as his *adlatus*.

This army, the increase and concentration of which became, we cannot say the cause, but the pretext or opportunity for war, at that moment occupied a line from Ivrea on the Dora Baiter down to its junction with the Po, thence on the left bank of this river as far as Casale and Valenza, and from this point across the hills to Alessandria on the Tanaro. It consisted of twenty regiments of infantry, ten battalions of *bersaglieri* or riflemen, eight regiments of cavalry, forming two divisions of heavy and one of light cavalry; and fifteen batteries of field artillery: in all, about 70,000 men. But this was not all; there were two bodies of volunteer riflemen—the Cacciatori delle Alpi under General Garibaldi, and the Cacciatori degli Appenini under Mezzocapo; and besides this, large depots in some of the regiments sufficiently strong to make up a new battalion.

The creation of this army had been the work of months, not to say of years; for ever since the disastrous campaign of 1819 the military organization of the country and the development of its warlike resources had been one of the chief and avowed objects of the successive governments. It had been entirely remodelled since that time, and had lost that exclusive class-colouring which formerly distinguished it, and no doubt contributed considerably to its failure ten years ago. As the Piedmontese army was to be the nucleus round which soldiers from all parts of Italy were to group themselves, it was felt that it could not remain so exclusively aristocratic, but must be popularized. Whatever has been done in this respect is generally and justly attributed to General La Marmora. By a patient process of years a *cadre* was thus formed on a sufficiently broad basis to include the elements from the rest of Italy, in case of an Italian war of independence.

The words of the emperor of the French on New Year's day opened out such a possibility,—nay, indicated its probability, and from that moment began a race between Austria and Piedmont, each taking the preparations of the other as a pretext for its own armaments. Scarcely had the sound of the words pronounced on New Year's day died away, when the Austrian official gazette announced the sending of a *corps d'armée* to Italy, the garrisons of Bologna and Ancona were reinforced, and a considerable force concentrated on the angle formed by the confluence of the Po and the Ticino. The gauntlet is taken up by Sardinia. On the 14th

TURIN—SARDINIAN CAVALRY PROCEEDING TO THE CAMP

all the army garrisoned in the different provinces is called together, and takes up a position between Casale and Alessandria, and almost at the same time the Sardinian Chambers are asked to sanction a loan of 50 millions of *francs*, in order to be prepared for emergencies, and a part of the money is expended in enlarging the fortifications of Casale and Alessandria. In March Austria sends a new *corps d'armée* (the fifth) to Italy, and Piedmont calls out her reserves. At the same time the agitation begins to tell all over Italy, but more especially in Upper and Central Italy. The "Italian National Society," which has formed itself under the presidency of Pallavicino, Garibaldi, and La Farina to promote the Italian movement, has, in spite of all precautions of the Austrian authorities and those of the Central Italian states, succeeded in establishing an understanding with all the most influential men, and by their exertions thousands of youths are able to come to Piedmont and enlist. In the month of March alone well-nigh 6,000 volunteers were enrolled by the commissioner specially appointed for that purpose in Turin, half of these being Lombards, the rest from Central Italy. Among these were numbers of youths belonging to the best families in Italy.

Thus from step to step the armaments increased on both sides, until, at the moment when hostilities were on the eve of breaking out, Austria had eight corps already in Italy and two more on the way; that is, she had 200,000 men, who in a short time were expected to be increased to 250,000; while the whole Sardinian force, volunteers and reserves included, must have been well-nigh 80,000 or 90,000 men under arms. Most of the volunteers who had come over were enrolled in the regular Sardinian army, only from 3,000 to 4,000 being left for the irregular corps.

But these 200,000 men, whom Austria had then in Italy could not, like most of the Piedmontese troops, be considered as an active army. For, besides the considerable garrisons which the number of strong places demanded, the general discontent forced the Austrians to employ at least one fourth of their armed force as garrisons to keep down the population of the numerous towns of Upper Italy. So that in the first instance, when they resolved to enter Piedmont, they could not muster more than six corps for their active army. These were the 2nd (Lichtenstein); 3rd (Schwarzenberg); 5th

(Stadion); 7th (Zobel); 8th (Benedeck); and the 9th (Schaffgotsch). The two remaining corps, the 6th and 11th, were left in the fortresses, furnishing garrisons for the towns of the Romagna, Venice and the other cities of that province, while the 1st and 10th were on their march from the frontiers of Austria. While Austria and Sardinia were thus, as it were, parading their armaments, there seemed scarcely any sign of preparations in France. Indeed, all insinuations in that respect were contradicted. That the army was not on a war footing when the hostilities broke out is certain, for with the exception of the regiments which came from Algeria, all the others had a considerable proportion of their men on furlough, and they arrived during the course of the campaign, some of them a short time before the Battle of Solferino. On the other hand, there is equally no doubt that large stores were heaped up in Marseilles several months before the war began. Besides this, there were strong suspicions at the time, of some of the war *matériel* having found its way into Piedmont before the war broke out. The conclusion to which one is driven, from these facts, is, that the military organization of France, even on a peace footing, is sufficiently complete to allow the sending-off, at a moment's notice, of an army of from 100,000 to 120,000 men; but that all the advantages given by railways and steam communications are not sufficient to dispense altogether with preparations made beforehand. But, although the contingency of a war was no doubt contemplated in France, it was not expected so soon, or else the people intrusted with the preparations were at fault; for the first troops sent off went as they stood, in many instances with less than thirty rounds of ammunition in their pouches. The artillery also was behindhand. It was intended to have nothing but the rifled guns of the new model of 1858; they were not ready in sufficient numbers, and some of the old guns had to be sent out to make up the complement of the artillery. The siege-train was equally unready, so were the train and transport departments. It will be remembered, that at the time Marshal Vaillant, then minister of war, was accused of negligence, and this accusation seemed to be confirmed by his removal from that post; but it is just as probable, that the sudden decision of Austria was the real cause of this state of half preparation.

But, whatever the cause, there was certainly no time lost in ap-

MONT CENIS—PASSAGE OF THE FRENCH

plying the remedy; and the energy and activity displayed in this respect were truly marvellous. It seemed as if a new spirit had penetrated everything, and no doubt this was the case, for from the first moment it was apparent that routine and bureaucracy had lost their sway, and that one man's energy directed everything. From all parts of France, the troops destined to form the five *corps* of the *armée d'Italie,* are carried by railway to Grenoble, Culoz, Toulon, and Marseilles—the four points on the frontier which were chosen for the concentration of the army. Both at Toulon and Marseilles war-steamers, and others belonging chiefly to the "Company of the Messageries Impériales," are ready to convey the troops to Genoa. From Grenoble and Culoz the regiments are sent in the direction of the passes of Mont Genèvre and Mont Cenis, and are ready to cross the frontiers at the first order. While the troops stationed in France are thus pushed forward in successive *échelons* towards the frontier, vessels are sent to Algeria—that ever ready camp of France—to fetch two complete divisions, and take them direct to the coast of Liguria. From the 21st of April this activity never ceases for about a month, and by that time the Imperial Guard, 10 divisions of infantry—that is, 52 regiments of the line, and 11 battalions of riflemen; 5 divisions or 20 regiments of cavalry, and 26 batteries of artillery, or 208 guns—were on Italian soil, besides an immense amount of stores and provisions, which were heaped up in Genoa, Alessandria, and Turin.

It was, as often happens in the beginning of warfare, a trial of speed with the adversary, but it was of greater moment on this occasion than usual. Not even the Piedmontese imagined themselves to be a match, single-handed, for the large forces which Austria had concentrated on their frontiers. The object, therefore, of the Austrians was clearly to crush the Piedmontese before their French allies could come up; and the endeavour of the Piedmontese, on the contrary, was to avoid, as much as possible, a general engagement until their trans-Alpine friends could arrive.

With this view the Piedmontese had long ago prepared a defensive position for their army. It is almost impossible to imagine a worse frontier-line for defence than that of Piedmont towards Lombardy. First, it formed a concave line, giving all the advantages of a central position to the aggressor; then this line was divided by the Po, making a concentrated system of defence difficult, if not impossible. Finally, it was outflanked by Piacenza long before this war was even thought of. The Piedmontese saw this evil, and looked for some more defensible position farther back: it was found in the angle formed by the confluence of the Po and the Tanaro.

Except towards the east, Piedmont is surrounded on all sides by a semicircle of mountains. The plain enclosed by this semicircle is divided almost in its centre by the river Po, which, rising in Mont Genèvre on the western frontier of Piedmont, runs in an easterly direction towards the Adriatic; but about the centre of the course through the Piedmontese plain, the Po makes a sudden bend to the south for about ten miles, after which it resumes again its easterly course. The river Tanaro, rising in the heart of the Appenines in the south, runs up to it at right angles to within a distance of fifteen miles; it then takes a parallel direction, in which it continues until it comes to the point where the latter makes its sudden bend to the south; then, after uniting with the Bormida, another of the streams of the Appenines, it runs up at a sharp angle towards the Po, joining it a few miles lower down. On the left bank, a little above the point where the Po makes its bend to the south, lies Casale; and at the confluence of the Tanaro and Bormida is built the fortress of Alessandria.[1] Casale, the ancient capital of the Marquisat of Montferrat, was once considered as the chief stronghold of the Ghibellines in this part of Lower Italy, while Alessandria was built by the Lombard League in the 12th century, in order to overawe Montferrat.

Both places fell and rose in importance, as peace or war prevailed in the plains of Upper Italy; and they regained all their former position when it became urgent, as in the times of the Lombard League, to form a stronghold and a focus of resistance against another foreign power from the North. These two fortresses in the centre of the country, not more than fifteen miles apart, and near the confluence of the two principal rivers into which all others flow at right angles, form together a position of great strength. Mutually protecting each other, and difficult of access on account of the rivers, all the military resources of the country can be con-

1. Both are names well known from the wars of the Guelfs and Ghibellineg, showing that even then their importance was understood.

centrated behind them, and then employed in any direction where a display of force may be required, while no enemy can pass them without exposing his line of retreat.

All these advantages had been long studied and understood by the Piedmontese, and no effort was spared to make Casale and Alessandria as strong as possible. Special grants of money were made by the Parliament for this object, and every one will still remember the subscription begun by Manin for the 100 guns of Alessandria; for Alessandria and Casale—no longer enemies, as in the days of the Guelfs and Ghibellines—were to be the *places d'armes* where all Italy could assemble and muster for the fight against the stranger. What gave additional importance to these two fortresses in the late war, was the necessity of protecting the roads by which the French army was to arrive,—namely, that over the Mont Cenis, and that from Genoa over the Appenines. With these fortresses on the two chief rivers as a base, any of the transverse rivers became a temporary line of defence, by which the Austrians could be kept in check until the French arrived. It was with this view that the Dora Baltea line was fortified on the road to Turin, and Novi on the Scrivia occupied, to ward off any attempt of the Austrians to close the defile of the Appenines.

This was the defensive position in which the Sardinian army was to wait for the arrival of its allies. In the hills of Montferrat, which lie between the Po and the Tanaro, protected in front and flank by these two rivers, having in Casale and Alessandria two *têtes de pont* from which to fall on the flank of an advancing enemy, the Sardinian army not only could avoid a general engagement with a superior enemy, but could likewise take advantage of any circumstance which might favour an offensive movement. To this *place d'armes*, then, the Sardinians had gradually sent their army battalion by battalion, and regiment by regiment, accompanied everywhere by the blessings and the enthusiasm of the people; so that when the Austrian ultimatum came, the main body of the Sardinian army was in this defensive position, with detachments at Chivasso on the Dora Baltea and at Novi on the Scrivia, to watch the road to Turin and the road to Genoa. The garrison of Genoa and Turin alone remained behind, while a few regiments of light cavalry were on the frontiers to observe the movements of the enemy; and they were to fall back slowly towards the rest of the army.

But while the Sardinian army had already occupied its defensive position, the defences themselves were by no means completed. The sudden resolution of the Austrians here showed its effect, and it was more than ten days after the Austrians crossed the Tieino before the works at Alessandria and Casale were finished.

The ultimatum of Count Buol is dated the 10th of April; it does not reach its destination until the 23rd, while its contents are known to the parties most nearly concerned so early as the 21st. The result made itself felt; before the memorandum was even presented, the railway had carried from 40,000 to 50,000 men to the Piedmontese frontier, and at least an equal number was concentrated in Marseilles and Toulon. Ten steamers of the Messageries Impériales were lying in the Joliette harbour, ready to take the troops on board. A number of the old paddle-wheel frigates, converted into transports, were close by, for similar purpose. Several line-of-battle ships and large transports were on their way to fetch the African divisions. Other transports, chartered for stores, were already loading with the greatest expedition. Thus, if there had been a time fixed not of three days, but of twenty-four hours, the French divisions, having already had a start of forty-eight hours, would have been equally in Sardinia at the end of that period. It was this delay between the writing and the presenting of the ultimatum which decided the race in favour of the allies, and not, as was said, the deference to the wish of England, in consequence of which the Austrian army only entered on the 29th.

By the 26th, when the period fixed by the ultimatum had elapsed, the French had had full five days to prepare, and before the Austrian envoy left Turin, with the answer to the ultimatum, two complete French divisions, Bazaine and Bouat, were already on Sardinian soil, the first at Genoa and the second over the Mont Cenis—that is, one only two hours from Alessandria by rail, and the other not so much from Turin. Now, supposing that the Austrians had availed themselves of the first moment to cross the Tieino, this could not have been very well done before the next morning, the 27th, Baron Kellersberg having left Turin only on the evening of the 20th; it would have taken their fleetest troops three days to march to Novi, or to the Dora Baltea, and by the 30th more than 60,000 French troops might have joined the Sardinian army. As for

GENOA—LANDING OF THE FRENCH TROOPS

reaching the Sardinian army before the French could come up, it was, therefore, no more to be thought of after the 26th, the day fixed for the answer to the ultimatum.

As soon as the Austrian ultimatum had been answered, no time was lost in Turin in making the last arrangements rendered necessary by the war. Already on the 23rd, at noon, that is, several hours before the Austrian ultimatum was presented, the Chamber, which had been prorogued for the Easter holidays, met on the sudden summons of the government; and on the proposal of the minister-president Cavour, conferred extraordinary powers on the King, investing him with full legislative and executive authority in case of war, and giving him power to take every measure necessary for the defence of the country, among the rest that of limiting individual freedom and liberty of the press during the time of war.

On the 26th, in pursuance of these extraordinary powers, a royal decree appoints three extraordinary civil commissioners, one for Genoa, another for Alessandria, and a third for Vercelli and Novara, with full powers, and dependent only on the commander-in-chief of the army, and the Minister of the Interior. The troops still left as garrisons in Turin and Genoa take their departure for the army, amidst the acclamation and good wishes of the people, and the national guard assume their duties. The king appoints the Prince of Carignan as lieutenant of the kingdom during his absence.

On the 27th, at ten a.m., a solemn mass is celebrated in the metropolitan church at Turin, to invoke the blessing of Heaven on the army. The king himself is present, as well as the Prince of Carignan, the ministers, the French embassy, the senators, most of the deputies, the magistrates, municipality, with functionaries of all degrees, officers of the army, as well as of the national guard, and a large assembly of people.

An immense crowd collects after the service on the Piazza del Castello, where the royal palace stands, waiting to see the king depart for the army, as had been announced the previous day. As there is no sign of an advance of the Austrians, the departure is deferred.

But Turin was not the only place in Sardinia which was in a fever of excitement on the 26th and the following days. The Austrian ultimatum being known, as well as the declaration in the *Moniteur* about the concentration of the five French *corps d'armée* on the Sardinian frontier, everyone was waiting anxiously for their arrival.

The Savoyards were the first who got a glimpse of them. There being as yet no railroad across the Mont Cenis, the troops had two days' march to make in Savoy, from St. Jean Maurienne until they came again to a railroad at Susa; it was therefore necessary for them to start sooner than those who were sent by Genoa. Already on the 25th, about noon, the first detachment of French troops arrived at the station of Chambery, amid the acclamations of the population assembled there since morning. The train contained the 19th battalion of Chasseurs-a-Pied and the 1st battalion of the 43rd of the line, both belonging to the 3rd *corps d'armée* (Canrobert). At four p.m. another train brought the remaining two battalions of the 43rd, and from that time every three hours another train passed the frontiers of Savoy on its road to the Mont Cenis; as the trains arrive at St. Jean Maurienne, the troops march on to the passage of the Mont Cenis, which is thus encumbered for days by long lines of troops, making their way across in spite of rain and snow, which are not wanting.

While this stream of French battalions is poured into Sardinia over the Mont Cenis, another stream passes by Mont Mélian; it is composed of the troops which have been concentrated at Grenoble and Briançon. Both unite at Susa, where the railway again begins.

By the time the first French battalions were effecting this passage over the Alps from the west, Genoa received within its walls the first detachment coming by sea. On the 26th, at eight a.m., the screw line-of-battle ship *l'Algésiras*, the steam frigates *Redoubtable* and *Dryade*, and the steam transports *Ulloa, Mogador*, and *Christophe Colomb* entered the port of Genoa. In the evening two more frigates and another transport followed; and before the next morning arrived, a division of six complete regiments, about 10,000 men, and their provisions had been landed.

The reception given to the troops at Genoa is very graphically described in a letter to the *Siècle* by M. Edmond Texier, which we here insert:

> I arrived at Genoa on the first day of the disembarkation, and I need not tell you that the city wore the appearance

Susa-Mont Cenis—Bivouac of French Troops

of a *fête*. This long-expected disembarkation had attracted an enormous crowd, drawn from all parts of Piedmont, and even from the neighbouring states. Everyone wished to be certain that the French had landed. The quays of this vast city of Genoa, which spreads in the form of a horse-shoe from the centre of the bay, its houses and palaces arranged in tiers one above the other, presented a noble spectacle. The terraces near the sea were crowded by women, who, with their heads covered by those long white veils called *posezolto*, waved handkerchiefs and scattered flowers below. Hundreds of boats were skimming out of the port to meet our ships, and each as it passed alongside discharged a volley of flowers upon our soldiers. It was enthusiasm approaching delirium. To every shout raised from the quays or the boats, the soldiers replied by cries of *Vive l'Italie!* and women, children, men old and young, wildly clapped their upraised hands,— like people shipwrecked, who, having given up all hope of deliverance, see the lifeboats coming to their rescue.

When the first frigate entered the harbour, the shouts broke into a universal *Vivat!* Italy felt herself liberated!

If ever enthusiasm was sincere, intense, pathetic, it was so at this moment. The whole population was in tears. 'Oh, Holy Virgin!' exclaimed an old woman, weeping as she spoke, 'they are then come!' and all the people around me wept also, as they shouted, *Vive la France! Vivent les soldats Français!* During the disembarkation the shouts never ceased, and the first soldiers who landed were literally stifled with embraces.

When the first French flag was lowered from the *Algésiras* into the boats, every head was uncovered, and all Genoa, by a spontaneous movement, bowed before the banner which had become the *labarum* of Italy. Even now Genoa wears the aspect of a French rather than of an Italian city. French uniforms are seen in every street, in every open place. Fifteen regiments of the line have already arrived, without counting Zouaves and Turcos. These last, with their swarthy faces and strange manners, are the lions of the hour. They are not quartered in the city like the other troops, but are encamped outside the gates, in the Polcevera valley.

In the evening, above all, Genoa presents a singular appearance. No one, seeing citizens and soldiers walking about arm in arm, would guess that this is a purely commercial city. At eight o'clock a hundred drums and bugles meet on the Piazza Ducale, and sound the "retreat." The people follow the drums, keeping step, and the drummers show redoubled vigour. Italian melodies mingle with French popular airs, cries of '*Viva la Francia!*' with those of '*Vive l'Italie!*' and from this confusion of sounds results a warlike enthusiastic harmony, which seems to breathe forth gunpowder, and is the presage of victory.

What is remarkable here, is the patriotic feeling of the people. Everyone has the same thought, the same object, and to attain it no sacrifice is deemed too great. The volunteers, who are mostly young men belonging to the best families of Italy, are drilling from morning till night, in the sun or in the rain, with an obstinate will, and they already manoeuvre like old troops. Some French officers who have been present at this drill tell me they should have no fear of acting with such allies. The Sardinian troops are full of ardour, and desire at any cost to repair the disaster of Novara.

One ought, to see this mighty rush of a whole people, to be convinced that the first want of Italy is independence.

And from this time an uninterrupted influx of troops continues from the west and the south. As fast as steamers and railways can carry them they arrive at Genoa and at the foot of the Alps, which they cross by forced marches. Those coming by sea encamp outside Genoa, while those coming over the Alps are concentrated at Susa and toward Pignerola in the country of the Waldenses. It was only in case of the greatest necessity that the detachments would have been sent immediately to the front, and that necessity did not exist up to the 29th, when the Austrians crossed. So that during three days, from the first arrival of the French troops on Sardinian soil, not only the divisions could be completed, but likewise many of the preparations made which could not be finished in the hurry of the departure. When the telegraph brought the news of the Austrian passage of the Ticino, there was always sufficient time to reach

THE RAILWAY BRIDGE OF VALENZA—AUSTRIANS BLOWING UP TWO ARCHES

the positions assigned to the different corps, to which they were closer than the Austrians. The French had also the use of railways, which the Austrians had not, after they had crossed the frontier.

We said the *armée d'Italie* consisted, of five corps and the imperial guard. Of these the 1st (Baraguay d'Hilliers) was composed of three divisions of infantry and one of cavalry; the 2nd corps (MacMahon), two divisions of infantry and one brigade of cavalry; the 3rd corps (Canrobert), three divisions of infantry and one division of cavalry; the 4th corps (Niel) three divisions of infantry and a brigade of cavalry; the 5th corps (Prince Napoleon), two divisions of infantry and a brigade of cavalry of the imperial guard, two divisions of infantry and two divisions of cavalry. Every infantry division was composed of four regiments of the line, each of three battalions, and a battalion of *chasseurs-à-pied*, in all thirteen battalions. With the exception of the regiments which had come from Algeria, very few of the battalions counted more than from 600 to 700 men, so that the divisions of infantry were from 8,000 to 9,000 men. The divisions of cavalry were formed of four regiments of four squadrons each, in all less than 500 horses. To each division, infantry as well as cavalry, a battery of artillery was attached, and the corps itself had as many batteries of reserve as it counted divisions.

Of this host, which, when completed, numbered fully from 150,000 to 160,000 fighting men, two-thirds came by sea to Genoa and one-third over the Alps. Although the original distribution of the *corps d'armée* was altered in some instances, it may be said that the six divisions of infantry and two of cavalry, forming the 3rd and 4th corps (Canrobert, Niel), came by the Alps. All the other divisions of infantry came by sea to Genoa. Before the evening of the 26th, 8,700 men were landed; by the evening of the 29th, 27,951 men and 990 horses; by the 1st of May, 51,000; and by the 16th of May, 87,000 men and 5,000 horses and mules. The official total of men landed being, before the end of the campaign, 113,075 men and 17,812 horses and mules.

Very few cavalry landed at Genoa, except a few regiments of *chasseurs*, the 2nd and 3rd, which came direct from Algeria, and 120 guides; all the rest of the cavalry, that of the imperial guard included, was sent by the Corniche. This passage across the Corniche was by no means favourable to the efficiency of this arm of the service, for owing to the ovations with which the cavalry was received all along the road, such care as the beginning of a campaign above all demands, seems not to have been paid to the horses; and the result was, that the cavalry of the guard had to leave from one-fourth to one-third of its horses, with sore backs, in the *depôts* near Genoa.

As for the landing of the troops, it was done well and rapidly: the huge *Bretagne* liner, for instance, discharged her 2,440 men, and sailed again in three hours. No doubt the facilities were great, there being a long line of new quays most of the way round the harbour, with water sufficiently deep for small ships; but all these advantages would have been lost, had it not been for the energy which was impressed on this whole movement, and the clear directions which seemed to guide this energy.

Not merely troops, however, were brought by sea, but the greater part of the military stores and provisions also came that way, and were heaped up in Genoa, which became the great centre of supplies. Connected by sea with Marseilles and Toulon, and by railway with Alessandria, Turin, and the line of operations in Piedmont, as well as in Lombardy, it was the most convenient place for that purpose. The town itself, with its storehouses and other commercial facilities, was, as it were, made for the purpose.

And in this great storehouse were laid up, it is calculated, six months' provisions for the whole army, and almost a year's for the cavalry.

Besides these provisions, the greater part of the siege artillery, reserve ammunition, gunboats in pieces,—in fact, everything which comes under the denomination of military stores, came to Genoa; although of pontoons and field artillery, not a little came by the Mont Cenis, by Grenoble, and by *Briançon*. But, on the whole, it could not escape attention that very little artillery passed in comparison with the number of troops, and yet there was the full complement of artillery in the field.

While the French army thus was concentrating at Genoa, and at the foot of the Alps, and the Piedmontese army was ready in its position between the Po and the Tanaro, the Austrians did not cross the Ticino before the 29th,—that is, three days after the ultimatum had been rejected by Sardinia. This is said to have been done in deference to the wishes of the British government.

This may be; but readiness to listen to such counsels evidently came from the conviction that a mistake had been committed, out of which, perhaps, the British government might show the way. Besides which, the Austrians had probably not been prepared for the rapidity with which the French had come up; their intention of crushing the Sardinian army before the arrival of its allies, was thus defeated; and so they did not know what to do. They had threatened to march into Sardinia, consequently they could not do less without losing all prestige from the very beginning, and yet they had no longer a hope of effecting anything if they did make this offensive movement. Under these circumstances, it was natural that they should listen to anything that offered some prospect of getting rid of the difficulty.

Being deceived in this hope, they took the resolution to cross the Ticino on the 29th in two columns, at Pavia and at Bereguardo. At the first of these two places the brigade Fistetics, of the 5th corps, was the first to pass, and it was followed by the entire 3rd corps (Schwartzenberg), the vanguard pushing on through Garlasco to the Terdoppio River, and the rest of the column remaining at Gropello. While this column passed at Pavia, the 7th corps (Zobel), coming down from Northern Lombardy to cross at Vigevano, found the bridge broken there, and had to pass on a pontoon bridge at Bereguardo, and march to Gambolo.

The same day, a detachment was sent across from Sesto Calende to Arona on the Lago Maggiore, to cut the telegraphic wires; which being effected, the detachment withdrew.

On the 20th, the 5th corps (Stadion) followed the 7th over the bridge of Bereguardo, and took its place at Gambolo, the 7th advancing to Mortara. The 8th corps (Benedeck) followed the 3rd by Pavia, both moving on to Garlasco. On the 1st of May the 2nd (Lichtenstein) followed these two last-named corps.

While the last troops had not yet crossed, the Austrian right already held Novara, the centre Mortara and the left San Nazzaro, that is, it was extended over a distance of 25 to 30 miles on the river Agogna, the second transverse river along the Po to Pavia.

The movements which follow from the 1st of May to the time of the advance of the allies at the end of the month, have greatly puzzled the world, and have given rise to the most extraordinary conjectures and supposed plans. And yet nothing was more simple; the events had only to be taken as they occurred, and no more importance attributed to them than they deserved.

The Austrians first take up a position in the angle made by the Sesia and the Po, they push forward in the direction of Turin, crossing the Sesia at Vercelli on the 2nd in force, while a small detachment crosses lower down at Caresana on the 3rd. On the same day they bridge over an arm of the Po at Cambio, they make a demonstration against Frasinetto, and have a cannonade with the Piedmontese at Valenza. On the 4th, the 8th corps (Benedeck) passes to the right bank of the Po, at Cornale, on a bridge constructed during the night by the engineers; they march to Voghera and Tortona, and blow up the railway bridge there. The bridge which Benedeck had made being carried away by the flood, he had to wait for the construction of a new one, which was ready in twenty-four hours, after which he retires, carrying with him a quantity of provisions, cattle, &c. Whilst this advance takes place on the right bank of the Po, the advance continues on the left bank. On the 5th, the Austrians bring a considerable force to Vercelli on the Sesia, and then push forward to Trino and Tobello, as well as Tranzaro and San Germano, and throw up works in this latter place and Vercelli. On the 7th, still larger bodies are sent towards Vercelli, and the movement extends towards Ivrea, on the Dora Baltea. On the 8th, the Austrians again make a movement towards Valenza, and blow up the railway bridge. On the 9th, a general movement of retreat begins. They evacuate Trino, Livorno, Tranzano, Santhia, &c.—in fact, all places on the right bank of the Sesia. Keeping merely a detachment at Vercelli, the bridges which they had constructed over the Sesia are again removed. On the 11th, a body of Austrians passes the Po at La Stella, and another detachment from Castel San Giovanni goes up the valley of the Trebbia. The 9th corps returns to Pavia. On the 12th, they establish themselves in force at Stradella and Castel San Giovanni. On the 13th, they occupy Bobbio, in the valley of the Trebbia, and rush on to Casteggio, on the road to Voghera. On the 14th, they retire from Bobbio. From the 14th to the 19th, they mass themselves on the road to Voghera, and fortify the bridge at La Stella. In the direction of the Sesia they make a requisition in the neighbourhood of Vercelli, and recross the Sesia, blowing up two arches of the railway bridge. On the 20th, they make a reconnaissance to Montebello, which ends in a defeat; after which they retire into their positions behind the Po and the Sesia, Gynlai transferring his headquarters from Mortara to Garlasco.

From this short *résumé* of the Austrian "operations" up to the combat of Montebello, it will be seen that the Austrians first take up a position right in front of that occupied by the Sardinians, between Casale and Alessandria; they make demonstrations against these two positions, and extend themselves to the right as if to gain the road to Turin; and then on the left, as if to advance against the defiles of the Appenines. They withdraw their left column and strengthen their right wing, massing large bodies there; then they withdraw those troops, again extend their left, and go on until they are beaten at Montebello.

It is clear that these operations were the result of no settled plan,—they were the manoeuvres of a blind man feeling his way first to the right and then to the left, until he comes against a wall. There is nothing very new and strange in this, for traces of it may be found at almost every page of the Austrian military history, that of the Archduke Charles not excepted. There never being a preference for doing anything in particular, a general reconnaissance is ordered, to make the enemy show his forces and develop *his* plan. It is this circumstance which causes so much divergence in the accounts of their operations, the Austrians calling that a reconnaissance which their enemies call a defeat.

While the Austrians were thus losing precious time, the allies exerted themselves to their utmost to concentrate their forces. With the exception of a few battalions belonging to the 1st French corps which were sent up to Novi in the valley of the Scrivia, not a man of the French army stirred until the telegraph brought the news of the advance of the Austrians. On the 29th, Marshal Baraguay d'Hilliers publishes his order of the day; and the 1st and 2nd corps cross the Appenines partly by rail and partly on the highroad, and are concentrated at Novi at the entrance of the Appenines. At the same time that the 1st and 2nd corps concentrate on the northern slopes of the Appenines, the 2nd and 4th corps, coming from the foot of the Alps, pass through Turin to the front. The first troops which reach the Sardinian capital on the 30th of April, are the objects of great ovations. Marshal Canrobert, and General Niel, have already arrived and have examined, in company with the King, the positions on the Dora Baltea, and on the Po.

The object, of course, could merely be to take such measures as would enable the allied armies to concentrate without being disturbed by anything the Austrians could undertake; with Alessandria as a flanking position, and the 1st and 2nd corps at the enhance of the defile of the Appenines, there could be not much danger of any interruption of the road to Genoa; so the chief attraction was toward the Mont Cenis road, especially as there seemed rather a tendency of the Austrians to push forward in that direction. With this view, the 3rd and 4th French corps were massed towards the centre of the allied position at Valenza, and the Sardinians were thus enabled to move more freely from Casale and watch the enemy's movements on that line, and towards the Dora Baltea. The retreat of the Austrians from their advanced positions in that direction relieved them from all further apprehensions, and the French army could now concentrate in all safety and prepare to take the offensive.

After the first few days, it had become tolerably clear that the Austrians had no hostile intentions, either in the direction of Genoa or of Turin; their operations did not produce much counter- movement in the allied armies, except when, for a moment, they occupied Bobbio, and the Zouaves were sent off in that direction; but reassured on this point, everyone was waiting impatiently the arrival of the emperor.

CHAPTER 2

The Combat of Montebello

The corps *législatif* having on the 2nd June voted the augmentation of the contingent for 1859 from 100,000 to 140,000, and sanctioned a loan of 500,000,000 *francs* by national subscription, the emperor next day conferred on the empress the dignity of Regent during his absence, and published a proclamation to the French people, in which he announced this resolution, and recommended her and his son to the care of the army remaining in France, and of the whole people. On the 10th, at five p.m., he left the Tuileries in an open carriage, accompanied by the Empress, and proceeded through a dense and enthusiastic crowd to the station of the Lyons railway. The Empress accompanied him as far as Montereau; and thence, almost without stopping, the imperial train proceeded to Lyons and Marseilles, where it arrived the next day. The emperor embarked at once on board the yacht *Reine Hortense*, and arrived in the afternoon of the 12th at Genoa.

The following two letters from the *Times* correspondent at this latter place give a graphic account of the emperor's reception.

Genoa, 17th May
At last all doubts and fears are set at rest by the actual arrival of Napoleon III. to take the command of the forces he has so rapidly thrown into this country. Long before any vessel neared the port, half Genoa, warned by a gun fired from the Lighthouse Battery, and the French tricolour floating out from the signal tower, was out on foot in the streets, or lined the road which runs round the port as far as the landing-place on the west side of our harbour, which for so many

days successively has presented the appearance of a disturbed anthill, or beehive, crowded as it has been daily with red-trousered bipeds, each armed with the sting that Austria is soon to feel.

At half-past one p.m., the *Reine Hortense*— originally the emperor's own yacht, but given by him to Prince Napoleon, on the occasion of the latter's marriage—slowly steamed in, and rounded to amid the thunder of royal salutes from the town. Her Majesty's steam-frigate *Terrible*, and several large French transports which arrived today, took up their positions in the deep water at the Old or Eastern Mole. At this moment the scene was very striking. As the smoke blew away, or lifted here or there, it opened vistas of manned yards and vessels draped in flags from truck to hull, and waving specks of every colour in the rainbow,—hats, shawls, and handkerchiefs,—while the deep roar of many thousand voices welcomed Napoleon to the land he comes to free.

The general effect of the arrival once observed, I jumped into a boat and hurried to the arsenal, to which a pass admitted me, that I might see the emperor 'set his foot upon the conquered shore.' Gaily-decked boats and ships, dressed in flags, formed a road which extended from the mole to the mouth of the arsenal, and along this, as I approached, was passing a handsome barge, bearing by way of figure-head what appeared to be a large gilt swan, evidently on its way to meet His Imperial Majesty. The arsenal itself presented a brilliant sight. The Imperial Guard were in full possession, lining the edge of the water as well as the battlements, with their tall fur caps, except at the landing-place, which, as the post of honour, was held by the Genoese Militia. A long line of chairs on the eastern side was occupied by ladies, apparently vying with each other in the splendour of their parasols; while a large vessel opposite heeled over, as I have seen Thames steamers do, with its freight of beauty, many a toilette fit for the most exclusive *salon* being mercilessly exposed to the chances of tarred rope and struggling crowd.

Shortly after my arrival renewed shouts warned us

GENOA—ARRIVAL OF THE EMPEROR NAPOLEON III

of the emperor's approach, and at ten minutes past two the barge I had before observed passed on towards the landing-place, now crowded with uniforms and decorated officers. The emperor sat where the steersman would do in an ordinary boat, between M. de Cavour and the Prince Carignan, and bowed repeatedly in acknowledgment of the enthusiastic shouts which greeted his appearance, and broke out again at the instant that his foot touched Italian soil. From the arsenal he passed at once by a covered bridge which crosses the Carlo Alberto Street, to the Royal Palace in the Strada Balbi, which belonged formerly to Girolamo Durazzo, the last Doge of Genoa, displaced by Napoleon I. in 1805, and was sold by his successors to the crown of Savoy. For the first time since the lauding of their allies, the Genoese seemed thoroughly excited, and for a short time lost that impassiveness they have shown throughout, which some say is caused by the instinctive mistrust of war natural to a commercial city; others by perfect satisfaction with the course events are taking. They cheered, and jumped up and down to see, and clapped their hands, and pushed for places with an eagerness instructive enough to one who observed that among the most enthusiastic were men of that party which but a few months ago sought the present hero's life. Let Napoleon keep his word, if he would go down a white-haired man to the grave, and seek to establish no French rule in Italy; for the present enthusiasm springs from hatred to the Austrian, not love to the Gaul, and the poniard which threatened him, though sheathed, is sharp as ever.

18th May
The opera *Ione* (of which the very effective *libretto* is founded on Bulwer's novel, *The Last Days of Pompeii*) began as usual at eight, to a crowded but sadly inattentive house, the theatre itself brilliantly lighted and decorated with the French and Sardinian tricolours. Soon after nine, and just before the ballet began, a general 'hush' running through the pit warned us of his Majesty's approach, and in a few minutes he appeared, and came forward at once to the front of the box, turn-

ing slightly pale, it seemed to me; showing thus an emotion which, if indeed it existed, can hardly have been caused by any doubt of his reception after what had passed during the day. At all events, the huzzas at the arsenal fade out of my mind when I think of the tremendous electrical shout that ran through the theatre, not given in regular time and for a definite object, as is our way in England, but each voice giving out its separate cry of '*Vive l'Empereur!*' '*Viva l'Italia!*' or '*Viva l'Allianza!*' and then cheering its own sentiment with '*Evviva, Evviva!*' repeated indefinitely. Every person in the theatre stood up, the ladies, three and four to the box, coming forward and waving their handkerchiefs; while the men behind them clapped their hands and cheered, compelling the emperor to come forward three times to receive their applause before the ballet was allowed to proceed. Napoleon sat in the centre of the box, which is not, like the royal box at Her Majesty's Theatre, merely distinguished by its size, but is admirably fitted to display its occupants, filling the centre of the second tier of boxes, and bulging forward in a semicircle into the house, supported on marble pillars which form the entrance to the pit, so that I had every opportunity of examining him carefully. On his Majesty's left were the Prince de Carignan, regent of the kingdom, and Count Cavour; on his right, Prince Napoleon and the French minister, De la Tour d'Auvergne; the royal personages only sitting, while the Syndic of Genoa stood behind their chairs. Once, in defiance of all etiquette, a voice cried, '*Viva Cavour!*' and a few cheers hailed the popular name; but the count gave a little start and shrink at the sound, and his friends in the royal box seemed to 'chaff' him on the subject.

I did not see the royal party leave the theatre, which they did at the end of the ballet; but here the exit was too rapid to allow of the display of much enthusiasm. I met them, however, on their way, about half-past ten, in the streets, splendidly illuminated along their whole course, and was much struck by the effect when the dull roar that preceded them burst into a shout like thunder, as they swept round the corner of the Via Nuovissima past me into the Piazza

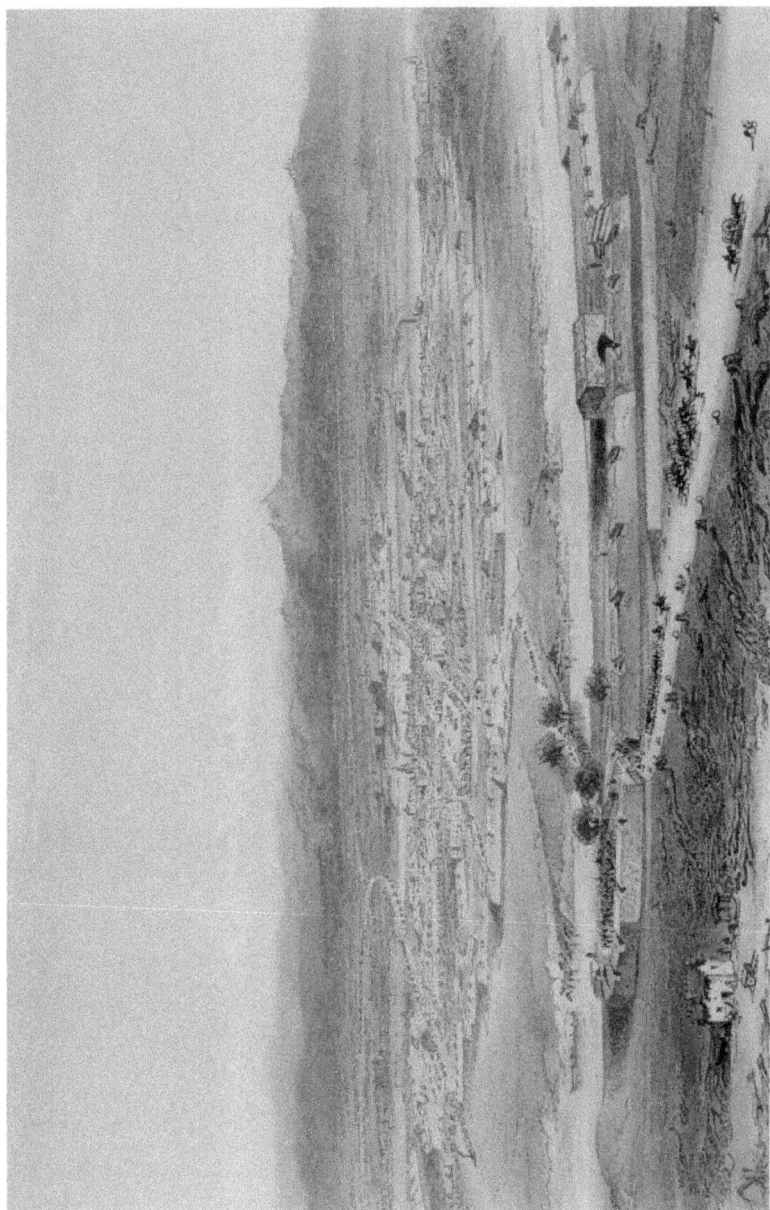

ALESSANDRIA AND ITS ENVIRONS

Annunziata, preceded and followed by splendidly-mounted gendarmerie, and disappeared, leaving comparative silence where they had been.

The town was glorious, indeed, last night; never had it worn such a gala dress since the marriage of the then Duke of Savoy in 1842. The streets, one blaze of flags and light, with golden garlands surrounding the favourite watchwords of Italian liberty, were thronged with Genoese citizens and French soldiers, a well behaved, intelligent, admiring crowd; while the churches seemed pinnacles of fire, raised in honour of their deity by worshippers of the sun; but there are those who will never forget Genoa, always beautiful, never more so than as it was seen from the sea last night. They will remember the amphitheatre of star-like houses rising silently from the sea, the strangely impressive sense of quiet and repose after the noisy streets and theatre, the Carignano church and the Lanterna on the extreme right and left, landmarks of the domain of light—the cathedral in the centre raising its bright front above its neighbours—the sea, smooth as glass, hardly breaking the lines of bright sparks and many-coloured lamps which it reflected; the clouds above, a grand foil to the shining city, all the darker for a gathering thunderstorm, which every now and then, by a single flash of lightning, seemed to show man that his utmost efforts were but a poor imitation of nature. Heavy rain, indeed, closed what guests and hosts alike must think a very successful day; but it did not come on till midnight, and then saved the use of an extinguisher.

The King of Sardinia came down from headquarters early this morning, stayed two hours, and returned. It is not known what Napoleon III.'s next movement will be.

On the day of his arrival at Genoa, the emperor addressed the army in an order of the day, in which he announced that he has come to put himself at the head of the army. On Saturday the 14th he left for Alessandria, where he arrived at four p.m., it would be endless to repeat amid the enthusiasm of the people, he established his headquarters at Alessandria, which from that moment became the focus and centre of all activity.

Even before this happened, the most superficial observer could see that all this movement of troops and material was directed by one mind and one will, that of the emperor at Paris; but it became much more the case after his arrival among the troops. He was the soul of everything; nothing was done without his sanction, even the minutest details being referred to him. Those details, which form, according to the organization of continental armies, the chief duties of the chief of the staff, were all under the personal direction of the emperor himself. It was probably with this view that Marshal Vaillant was chosen for the post, there not being much chance of his doing anything without authority. It was this which brought such a unity and precision into everything as were rarely before attained in any campaign. The great engine for this centralization was the use of the electric telegraph. There was a regular telegraph department attached to each *corps d'armée*, carrying wires, poles, and instruments with it, and having a certain number of sappers at its disposal. Whichever way the *corps d'armée* advanced, the telegraph followed immediately; if it changed its direction and the telegraph became useless, it was taken down, and put up where it was required. Thus all conflicting messages, mistakes of *aides-de-camp*, &c..were avoided, and a rigid and clear means of communication established with headquarters.

By means of these electric wires the emperor from Alessandria moved this mass of men and *matériel*. One must have seen an army of from 100,000 to 150,000 men, with all its numerous wants, in order to form a correct idea of the work required to make it movable; and in this campaign there were wants which do not commonly occur. First, the numerous rivers which intersect the plains of Upper Italy in every direction required an unusual pontoon train, and special care had to be bestowed on this department, which in ordinary campaigns forms a quite subordinate part of the *matériel*. The rapidity with which the rivers were bridged during the advance of the army, and the almost complete absence of accidents, proved that the dispositions made beforehand were equal to the requirements. Then there was the siege train, which, intended as it was against the formidable quadrilateral, had to be disproportionately large; and the gunboats, which had to be prepared and sent out for the Lago di Garcia and the Mincio.

ARRIVAL OF THE EMPEROR NAPOLEON III AT THE PALACE, ALESSANDRIA

But besides these extraordinary requirements, the ordinary wants for the mobilization of so large a force were enormous. The first thing was to organize an auxiliary train for the army. This was done by contracts with private individuals, who supplied the carts of the country. As the army was not to live on requisitions, everything had to be brought from France, with the exception of fresh meat, which was contracted for. Add to this, that while these preparations were made for the future, the army had to be fed from day to day, and one cannot but admire the talent of the man who directed all these different efforts towards their common aim.

This was, however, only possible by the assistance of the telegraph, the railways, and the steam communication by sea. All these inventions were for the first time applied to warfare on a large scale, and certainly there never was a more complete success achieved on a first trial. It is the more surprising, as some of these means were in an imperfect state; for instance, on most railways there was but one line of rails, the stations were far too small, and the *matériel* rather scanty; yet, in spite of this, the railway did wonders, and without an accident during the campaign. It was when everything was over that the only accident occurred, between Turin and Susa.

This colossal stir and movement of men and stores, which now appears so well directed, presented at the time to the spectator the most hopeless scene of confusion. A train with pontoons passing one way meeting another laden with guns passing in an opposite direction,—here one with a battalion of infantry—there another with guns and projectiles—a third loading with cavalry horses—a fourth with provisions; and so on, day and night.

In the midst of this activity occurs the combat of Montebello.

By the time the emperor arrived in Alessandria the mass of the French army had taken up its position in front, to the right of the Sardinian army, which, as has been explained, withdrew at the approach of the Austrians into its position behind the Po and Tanaro, between Casale and Alessandria. As the French divisions arrived one after another, the Sardinian army concentrated on its own left about Casale, Frassinetto, and the hills of Montferrat behind them. The fourth French corps coming from the west took its position between Valenza and Bassignana, on the point where the Tanaro joins the Po. The second corps (MacMahon) to the right of the fourth, extended from the right bank of the Tanaro through Sale to the left bank of the Scrivia at Castelunovo Scrivia; the first corps (Baraguay d'Hilliers) again to the right of this, from the Scrivia to the spurs of the Appenines at Voghera and towards Castellaro; the third corps was behind the first as reserve at Pontecurone, while the Imperial Guard at Alessandria formed the general reserve. The king's headquarters were at San Salvatore.

The allied armies thus occupied a position along the bend of the Po, on the right bank of it, from Casale to the foot of the Appennines, embracing as it were the Austrian army, which was on the left bank, holding the inner line along the bend.

The Austrian general, having given up his offensive intentions, if he ever entertained any, was now only intent on discovering at which side the allies would make their own offensive movement. In order to ascertain this, Count Stadion of the 5th corps was ordered to move forward from Stradella towards Voghera. Besides two brigades of his own corps, he had two others, forming General Urban's flying division, placed under his command, in all about 20,000 men, with whom he was to move forward towards Voghera until he met the enemy in force.

Accordingly, he started in the morning of the 20th of May from Stradella. The two brigades of General Urban forming the left column advanced by the main road towards Casteggio, while the brigadier-general of the 5th corps, leaving this road, went to the right towards Casatisma, on the road from Casteggio to Pavia, and the brigade of Gaal (5th corps) was still farther to the right towards the village of Branduzzo. The Austrian reconnaissance was thus advancing in a line between the spurs of the Appenines, which the main road to Voghera skirts, almost to the banks of the Po.

The French had their videttes in advance of Montebello;[1] they consisted of Sardinian cavalry. The Austrian division Urban, passing through Casteggio by eleven a.m., advanced on Montebello. The Sardinian cavalry fell back towards Ginestrello, trying to re-

1. Mr. Bossoli's sketch represents the moment of the attack on the village of Montebello, which is seen on the height, as well as the country to the left, and Casteggio behind.

PANORAMIC VIEW FROM S. SALVATORE—HEADQUARTERS OF THE KING OF SARDINIA

tard the advance of the Austrians. The Sardinian cavalry, consisting of the regiment of Montferrat, and some squadrons of other regiments, in all 800 to 1,000 men, under the command of General Sonnaz, on this occasion made some brilliant charges, which somewhat retarded the advance of the Austrians, and gave time for the division Forey to come up. By the time that General Urban had debouched from Ginestrello, the first brigade of General Forey's division was on the spot. At the outskirts of the village of Ginestrello, towards Voghera, runs the little stream Fossagazzo; this had been the limit of the French outposts, and was occupied by two battalions of the 84th regiment; these battalions occupied the banks of the stream on both sides of the main road, and were soon joined by two battalions of the 74th, which General Forey brought up, together with a battery of artillery. This latter having taken a position on the road, one of the battalions of the 74th was sent to the left, towards the railway line; the Sardinian cavalry was likewise sent to the left.

This battalion of the 74th, under Colonel Cambriels, and the Sardinian cavalry, became the object of renewed attacks on the part of the enemy. They, however, kept their ground bravely, the Piedmontese cavalry by its brilliant charges, repeatedly checking the columns of the Austrians, and the battalion of infantry receiving them in turn with a well-directed fire. General Blanchard, with the 2nd brigade of the division Forey, arrived just in time to put an end to this unequal fight. As soon as this reinforcement had turned the left, the village of Ginestrello was taken, after considerable resistance. This being done, the first brigade was sent to the right of the road on the slopes of the Appenines, towards Montebello, and occupied one of these slopes; while the artillery, protected by the Piedmontese cavalry, advanced towards the same point by this road. The second brigade was left *en échelon* to the left of the road, to watch the movements of the Austrians in that direction. By half-past six the village of Montebello was carried, and the Austrians were falling back in every direction.

Each side had lost about 1,200 or 1,500 men in dead and wounded, for which the French got in exchange a few prisoners and empty ammunition-waggons. Already in this first engagement great want of discretion on the part of the Austrians was apparent in leaving the division of General Urban to its fate, without trying to extricate it. The other division of the 1st French corps complained that on their side, too, more might have been done, for they could have been brought up so as to take part in the engagement. That it was not done, was attributed to the wish on the part of Baraguay d'Hilliers to give General Forey an opportunity to clear himself of any imputation which might have remained on him since the Crimean campaign; the more probable cause seems to have been the orders of the emperor not to risk hastily a general engagement.

The Battle of Montebello

CHAPTER 3

The Battle of Palestro

The "reconnaissance" of Montebello was the last attempt on the part of Gyulai to ascertain the plans and intentions of the allies. It must have been quite satisfactory, for, from that moment, he was persuaded that the allies intended to make their offensive movement on his left, and he consequently massed his army on that side. Already on the 19th he abandoned Vercelli and withdrew his outposts to the left bank of the Sesia. He had scarcely done so when the division Cialdini, which had been watching the movements of the Austrians along the Sesia, entered Vercelli. On the 21st the same division forded the Sesia in two columns, and established its outposts on the left bank of that river. This was the first offensive movement on the part of the allies, the first step for carrying out the plan of the emperor. This plan he himself explains in his bulletin of the 5th of June, which says:

> The French army, massed round Alessandria, had great obstacles to overcome. If it marched on Piacenza, it had to besiege that place and force the passage of the Po, which is, at that point, 900 *mètres* broad; and this difficult operation had to be carried out in the face of an army of more than 200,000 men.
>
> If the emperor passed the river at Valenza, he found the enemy concentrated on the left bank at Mortara, and he could not attack it in this position, except by separate columns manoeuvring in a country intersected by canals and rice-fields. There was, consequently, on both those points an obstacle almost impossible to overcome; the emperor,

consequently, decided to turn it, and 'he gave the change' (*donna le change*) to the Austrians by massing his army on the right, and by occupying with it Casteggio and even Bobbio on the Trebbia.

To execute this turning movement of which the emperor speaks, it was determined to concentrate the whole army, with the exception of a few detachments remaining in Alessandria and Casale on the extreme left of Vercelli, which corresponded to the extreme right of the Austrians. As soon as this concentration was effected, the Sardinian army was to advance from Vercelli in the direction of Mortara, so as to strengthen the belief of the Austrians in an attack on that side; and under the protection of this feint the French army was to pass the Sesia and march on Novara, taking up a position on the right rear of the Austrians; forcing them thus to abandon their position on the Po, and either to accept a battle under the greatest disadvantages—that is, with their line of retreat on their right flank—or else to recross the Ticino. In order still more to deceive the Austrians, and everyone else, the rumour was spread of an advance towards Voghera, and the military household of the emperor was several times sent to the railway-station in Alessandria ready for departure, and again stopped by simulated counter-orders.

In the mean time, the concentration on the left had begun on the 28th. On that day, the division Cialdini, which had until then only outposts on the left bank of the Sesia, established itself altogether on that side; and under its protection French engineers began to construct two bridges, one above and the other below the railway bridge, which had been blown up by the Austrians. The same day the infantry of the corps of Marshal Canrobert (3rd) which was in second line at Pontecurone, was transported by rail to Alessandria, and from thence to Casale; while the artillery, baggage, and cavalry followed by forced marches. On the 29th, of the four Sardinian divisions which, it will be remembered, were still at Casale, three went to Vercelli, while the fourth was left as garrison in that fortress. The third French corps which had arrived the day before, followed on the road to Vercelli as far as Stroggiana, and then turned towards Pravolo, in the direction of the Po. In the place of these troops, the infantry of the guard arrived the same day at

TORTONA—FROM THE RIVER SCRIVIA

The Piedmontese Army crossing the Sesia

Casale, by rail, from Alessandria, and the fourth corps (Niel) from Valenza and Bassignano by the road. The place of the fourth corps was taken by the second, which advanced from Sale and Castelnuovo Scrivia; the first from Voghera moved down to Tortona and Alessandria. Casale, which had been before the extreme left of the position, became thus, as it were, the pivot of the whole movement, round which the army moved partly by rail and partly on the road by forced marches.

On the 30th, the Sardinian army, with the exception of the division which was left at Casale, crossed the Sesia on the only bridge which the engineers had been able to construct until then, the others having been unsuccessful, owing to the sudden flooding of the rivers. The object of this advance was to "give the change" to the Austrians, as the emperor says. The Sardinian army had to drive the Austrian detachments from Palestro and Vinzaglio, the two points where they had their outposts towards the Sesia. While this was being done, the fourth corps (Niel) coming from Casale, was to cross the Sesia likewise at Vercelli, and advance on the road of Novara to Borgo Vercelli. At the same time the third corps at Pravolo was to pass at that place on pontoon bridges, and form a reserve for the Sardinian army, if it should be attacked by superior forces.

The Imperial Guard advanced on the same day from Casale, on the road to Vercelli, but encamped in the rear of Pravolo; the second corps marched through Casale on the traces of it; and the first corps went that day, partly by rail and partly by the road, to Casale. Thus by the 30th, or *two days* after the movement had begun, the whole army was massed on what had been its left. It occupied the line of the Sesia from Vercelli down to its confluence with the Po.

The three points, Vercelli, Mortara, and Novara, form an isosceles triangle, of which Mortara is the apex. The moment, therefore, the Sesia was crossed, the allies were nearer to Novara than the Austrians at Mortara. Even if the Austrian army had been concentrated at this latter place, it would have been too late to protect the Ticino at Novara. But the Austrian commander, being under the impression that the allies would force the passage of the Po between Piacenza and Valenza, had concentrated all his forces in that direction, leaving only the seventh corps (Zobel) at Mortara, with its outposts towards the Sesia. The most advanced of these outposts held the two villages of Palestro and Vinzaglio, both on the road from Borgo Vercelli to Robbio and Mortara; and against these points the Sardinian army advanced on the afternoon of the 30th, the anniversary of the Battle of Goito.

The whole of the Lomellina is one mass of corn and rice fields, divided from each other by raised causeways and ditches of three or four feet, which serve for the purpose of irrigation. On the borders of these divisions between the fields are closely-planted trees, mostly poplar and plane, while the fields themselves are studded with mulberry-trees. The corn, the growth of which is very luxuriant, was just in full bloom, offering good cover for riflemen; the rice-fields, on the contrary, were just peeping out of the water. To distribute the water equally, little raised banks are thrown up, according to the level of the ground, in serpentine lines. The roads are artificial embankments, kept considerably above the level of the fields; the by-roads mostly bad, but not impassable even for artillery. Both the villages of Palestro and Vinzaglio are on the first rise above the low banks of the Sesia. This rise, as all those on the river-banks of Upper Italy, is so sudden, as to look almost like an artificial embankment, through which the roads are cut. The Austrian outposts had barricaded themselves at the entrance of the village. According to their own account, there were four companies and four guns in Palestro, and two companies and two guns at Vinzaglio, which seems rather a strong proportion; however, the force certainly was not more than 2,000 men, and, at any rate, not one calculated to resist the Sardinian army.

The dispositions were, that the advance should be made in three columns:—the 4th division, Cialdini, on the main road to Palestro; the 1st division, Durando, on the road to its left, to march on Vinzaglio; and the two other divisions, Fanti and Castelborgo, still further left, to go by Casalino to Confianza, and move down from thence on a cross road on Vinzaglio, so as to open the road to Durando's division, which, in its turn, was to take Palestro in flank—that is, the whole was a combined flank movement from the left, to cut off the Austrian outposts. It failed; and Cialdini had to take Palestro by force. He sent a section of artillery forward on the road, followed by one of his brigades; the other was sent to the right, in order to penetrate at the Ponte Montreoli, over a canalized arm of

Attack of Palestro—by the Fourth Piedmontese Division (Cialdini)

Attack of Ponte Montreoli, Palestro—By the. Brigade Regina, Fourth Division

the Busca. Both attacks succeeded almost at the same moment, and the Austrians were driven out of the village. Beyond the village, to the left of the road to Robbio, is the cemetery; behind this the Austrians tried to form and protect their retreat. For this purpose they opened fire with their artillery on the Piedmontese column, which tried to debouch from the village; they gained thus time to effect their retreat. While this was passing at Palestro, Durando arrived at Vinzaglio, where he met with little resistance, the Austrians falling back towards Palestro. Soon after this latter had been taken, they were again seen approaching, a detachment was sent against them; but without awaiting the arrival of this latter, the Austrian column made for the fields, leaving its two guns on the road. These two guns and 120 to 150 prisoners were the trophies of the fight for the Piedmontese.

While the fight was still going on, the emperor arrived at Vercelli by railway, from Alessandria. In spite of the rain which had lasted since the morning, a considerable crowd had collected at the railway-station, and cheered him heartily on his arrival. Almost immediately after his arrival he went to the battle-field. Even before going there, the 3rd Zouaves belonging to the 5th corps (Prince Napoleon) but now on detached duty, were sent across the Sesia to take up a position on the right rear of the Sardinians at Palestro. The object of this measure was to protect the extreme right against any column which might come up in that direction, and thus impede the passage of Canrobert's corps at Pravolo. This corps had not yet been able to pass, owing to the floods of the Sesia, which prevented the construction of bridges. The emperor returned after sunset to Vercelli, and in the evening the place was illuminated. The emperor walked through the town, being as usual the object of great ovations on the part of the people, as well as of the soldiers.

The next morning the Imperial Guard as well as a part of the 2nd corps arrived at Vercelli. The Sesia had fallen considerably, and it was then possible to construct the bridges at Pravolo, and to repair the road at Vercelli which had been carried away by the Hood. While every effort at Vercelli was concentrated in making bridges and moving the troops across, the Piedmontese army was to have made a movement in the direction of Robbio, in order still more to divert the attention of the Austrians from the real object of the allies.

But just when the Piedmontese army was preparing to advance in two columns, one from Palestro, and another from Confianza, it was attacked in its turn by the Austrians. The advance of the Sardinians the day before, seems to have rather alarmed General Gyulai, and he ordered two of his corps, the 3rd and 2nd to come up towards Mortara that very night, while General Zobel received orders to retake Palestro and Vinzaglio. He had not his whole corps together, only two brigades of it; to these was joined a division of the 2nd corps, making in all four brigades, with which he advanced in three columns—the main column by the road from Robbio on Palestro, another to the right on Confianza; and again, another on the left, coming from Rivoltella, was to attack Palestro from the right, and threaten the communication with the Sesia. The Piedmontese division Cialdini (4th) was in position in rear of Palestro, towards Robbio. About 600 yards from the village there is a slight elevation in the ground, followed by a corresponding depression; this was chosen as the position for the night of the 30th, and some light field-works constructed on it. The brigade Regina *à cheval*, on the road to Robbio, occupied this position in advance, and detached some companies to the right to watch the road which comes from Rosasco and Rivoltella, parallel with the Sesia, to Palestro, especially the bridge della Brida, over which one of these roads crosses the canal of the Sartirana. The other brigade formed the second line in rear of the first. The 3rd regiment of Zouaves, which had been placed by the emperor at the disposal of the king, arrived about eight a.m., from Torrione, where it had passed the night, and took up a position to the right of the road from Palestro to the Sesia.

About ten a.m. the Austrians appeared before the position at Palestro. The ground being thickly covered with trees, and the corn just ripening, the Austrian columns could advance without being perceived. The brigade Dorndorf, which came by the main road, finding the attack by the road rather difficult, on account of the fieldworks and the elevation of the ground, made its chief effort on the flanks of the Sardinian position, and succeeded in driving back the Sardinians, placed to the left of the road; it had almost succeeded in doing the same on the right, when timely reinforcements checked the Austrian advance on that point. While

The Battle of Palestro—The King of Sardinia leading the troops

AUSTRIANS DRIVEN INTO THE ROGGIONE CANAL, SARTIRANA

this passed in front, the Austrian column, coming from Rosasco, on the by-road, had driven away the Sardinian outposts from the bridge della Brida, and advanced over it towards the Cascina San Pietro. This latter was quickly taken, and the column went on towards the right of the village. The intention was clear enough: it was to gain the road to the Sesia, and thus cut off the retreat of the Sardinian troops at Palestro. The 7th Bersaglieri were sent to the right, in order to check their advance; for a moment they retook the Cascina San Pietro, but lost it again; a second attempt, in which the 1st battalion of the 16th regiment participated, was not much more successful, and things began to look very critical. It was at that moment that the 3rd Zouaves, who had been encamped to the right rear of the village, were called into action. The road from Rosasco to Palestro, on which the Austrian brigade Szabo was advancing, is a raised causeway, which runs at almost right angles to the road from Palestro to the Sesia. Thus, the Zouaves, who were encamped to the right of this road, were on the flank of this column.

At the first sound of cannon and musketry the Zouaves were under arms, but it was only when Szabo's brigade advanced that they moved. They were separated from this latter by an open space of ground of a few hundred yards, and had just in front of their position a canalized branch of the Sesia, commonly called Canale della Cascina, about three feet deep. The bugle sounded the advance, and on the Zouaves went with an *élan* which astonished friend and foe. Pushing through the canal in front, they advanced *en pas de course* along the open space towards the Austrians. These, seeing an enemy suddenly start out where they least expected, turned three guns in that direction, which, however, did not stop the Zouaves for an instant; they were among the guns before the artillerymen could fire off their last shot. So quick was the rush and so rapid the pace, that the Zouaves arrived at the guns *pêle-mêle* with the Tyrolese *chasseurs*, who had been in skirmishing line before the guns. On the other side of the causeway were two other guns, which fell likewise into the hands of the Zouaves. The brigade Szabo was now rushing back towards the bridge della Brida, which is at the point where the sluice is for raising the water from the canal. The Zouaves, the 7th Bersaglieri, and the

69

16th Infantry regiments, rushed after them, and reached them at the bridge, over which they had not yet had time to retreat. The havoc here was terrible, for numbers were thrown into the canal, and drowned. The three guns, with which the Austrians had tried to protect the passage over the bridge, fell into the hands of the Zouaves and Sardinians. The defeat of this column decided the retreat of all the Austrian columns, for their combined movement could no longer be carried out, especially as the column by Vin-zaglio had been likewise checked, and the centre had now to look to its own safety. By two p.m. the Austrians had disappeared, leaving eight guns and about eight hundred prisoners in the hands of the allies, besides several hundred drowned in the canal or slain on the battle-field. The victory was purchased rather dearly by the allies, for the Zouaves alone had 350 men *hors de combat*, and the Sardinians not less than 800 or 1,000.[1]

But it was not the trophies gained by the allies which gave the battle of Palestro its importance,—it was the circumstance that it decided the success of the flank movement: for, while the Austrian columns were retreating precipitately, the French columns passed the Sesia, and gained the road of Novara. The Sesia had fallen considerably, and all difficulty about the bridges was thus removed. Canrobert's corps had passed the night before at Pravolo, and a part of the 2nd corps had likewise crossed at Vercelli. The 4th corps, which had been already the day before at Borgo-Vercelli, advanced to Orfengo, half-way to Novara. The 1st corps was approaching from Casale, and part of it was at Vercelli the same day. This passage over the Sesia was one of the most animated scenes imaginable; the Battle of Palestro, which inaugurated the advance of the allies, acted like a stimulant on the soldiers, giving them twice as much spirit and willingness. They had some hard marching—at any rate, part of them; but there were no stragglers or trace of sore feet, which scarcely ever fail when a campaign is opened by a forced march before the soldier is in marching condition.

The next morning, the 1st of June, the *avant-garde* of the 4th corps had entered Novara, after exchanging a few shots with the small detachments which the Austrians had there. A curious story

---

1. M. Bossoli's sketches give an excellent idea of the two great episodes of the Battle of Palestro—the charge of the Zouaves and the Austrian retreat over the Sardinian canal.

AUSTRIANS DRIVEN INTO THE ROGGIONE CANAL, SARTIRANA

was current in the 4th corps about this advance, which proves how little idea the Austrians had of the approach of the Allies. At one of the cross-roads a few miles before the town, a Tyrolese *chasseur*, having put aside his rifle, was quietly mending his trowsers, which he had taken off for the purpose. It was in this state that an advanced French cavalry-picket came down upon him and took him prisoner.

The same afternoon the Imperial Guard passed the Sesia, on the road to Novara, whither the emperor likewise transferred his headquarters. Day and night troops, stores, baggage, provisions, crossed the bridge on the Sesia, and the whole road from Vercelli to Novara was for two days, the 1st and 2nd of June, an almost uninterrupted mass of human beings, quadrupeds, and carts, which, like a long procession of ants, moved slowly in one direction.

Novara the sober, Novara the quiet, was scarcely to be recognized with these thousands and tens of thousands of new guests. Although, with the exception of the Imperial Guard, encamped outside of the town, they invaded it immediately after their arrival, in search of tobacco and other little dainties, it was indeed astonishing, after their march in the hot sun for several days, to see them running about the streets instead of indulging in repose after their fatigue; but everything had been so successful, that none felt weary, and already the soldier began to have a kind of superstitious confidence in the star and skill of his emperor.

Chapter 4

The Combat at Turbigo

By the 2nd of June the success of the great strategic movement of the allied armies was decided. The 1st, 2nd, 3rd, and 4th
French *corps d'armée*, in all little less than 100,000 fighting men,
were massed in the plain to the south-east of Novara, on the very
spot were the last shot had been fired in the campaign of 1849,
so disastrous for the army of Sardinia and for the cause of Italy.
This powerful body fronted to the south, thus threatening the
flank of the Austrian position at Mortara, and at the same time
protecting the chief passage across the Ticino, over the bridge
of Buffalora. Behind this barrier of bayonets the Sardinian army,
which had hitherto masked the whole movement, could without
apprehension withdraw along the road to Novara, and take up the
position assigned to it on the Ticino, north of Novara. All danger
was now over; for if the Austrians attempted to disturb its retreat,
they exposed their right flank to an attack by the main body of
the French army, and ran the risk of losing their line of communication over the Ticino.

The favourable moment had passed away, to return no more; for
in war, as in a game of chess, all depends on a single move at the
right moment,—he who misses it is checkmated. With more than
usual luck, the Austrians had well-nigh three days, during which
they might have broken through the combinations of the allies, and
turned the scale in their own favour. Three days, from the 30th of
May to the 1st of June, during which the French army was thronging over three bridges across the Sesia, which had considerably
swollen, owing to the rains. Nay, the very first day of the passage,

PIACENZA—AUSTRIANS CROSSING THE RIVER PO

Charge of the Piedmontese Chevaux-Legers at Ginestrello

one of the bridges was carried away by the flood, and the others were in imminent danger of sharing the same fate. All this time the Austrian army, concentrated at and before Mortara, was but a few leagues distant, and had only the Sardinian army in front of it, and such parts of the 3rd French *corps d'armée* as had already passed over. If then, instead of amusing themselves with a desultory attempt to retake Palestro, they had pushed forward with their whole strength, the chances were that they would have broken through the troops opposed to them and cut the allied army in two.

But so little had the Austrians been aware of what was passing on the other side, that, according to a letter of the 29th of May from *The Times* correspondent at Austrian headquarters, they were wondering at the incomprehensible inactivity of the allies, at the very moment when the greatest part of their army was already on the Sesia, and when the bridges over that most capricious of rivers were already completed, or in process of construction. The first idea which the Austrians seem to have had of some movement on the part of the allies was the appearance of the French troops at Novara on the 1st of June, when it was already too late to make any counter-movement. It is difficult to understand how they came to be so completely outwitted. No single cause could produce such a result, and a concurrence of circumstances must be supposed to explain so rare an instance of a strategical defeat. First among these must be placed the remarkable skill with which the movement was effected by the allies. The idea itself, as well as the manner in which it was realized, will bear comparison with the most striking strategical combinations of the best generals of ancient as well as modern times, while in boldness it surpasses most of them.

By taking the initiative, the Austrians had secured to themselves all the advantages of a strategical position. With Piacenza to guard their rear, the Po on their left flank, and the Sesia in front, they were in a kind of natural stronghold between the Sardinian army guarding Turin, and the French army collecting on the right bank of the Po, able to come down on either with full strength if it attempted to cross. It was probably this very good position which made them careless about the movements of the enemy, sure as they were that he must come their way,—that is, across the Po or the Sesia. By the concentration of the French corps on the road to Piacenza and the Po, they were led into the belief that the chief effort of the allies would be made there; and after the reconnaissance, which history will call the defeat, of Montebello, they concentrated a large part of their troops on the banks of the Po, in the direction of Pavia and Piacenza. Thinking themselves safe, and at the same time having made up their mind from which side they would be attacked, they took the advance of the Sardinians for a feint to facilitate the crossing of the Po by the French army, and never imagined that, while they were preparing for the real attack of the French on the Po, the whole French army had marched, in three days, from the extreme right of their position at Voghera to Vercelli on the Sesia; and that, while they made a useless effort to give a lesson to the Piedmontese at Palestro, the French army was fast getting massed on their right flank.

Besides this, the intelligence department of the Austrians seems to have been from beginning to end most miserably managed. According to their own officers, they never knew anything of what was passing at the other side. This may have been an excuse; but how can this ignorance be reconciled with the great love and willingness of the people of the Lomellina, who, according to Austrian accounts, were doing wonders to save Austrian corps from destruction by the river Po? With this willingness to expose their lives to save the 8th corps from the rapid river, there ought surely to have been no difficulty in finding men willing to cross over to the allied side, and bring back information.

But even later, when they were on the Mincio, in their own country, we see them attributing the failure of the Battle of Solferino, in great measure to the circumstance of their not knowing that the French were in force at Castiglione. Thus we cannot but come to one of two conclusions—either their intelligence department was badly managed, or else they complained of it in order to extenuate their other mistakes. At any rate, the skill with which the flanking movement was executed on the part of the allies, the ignorance of the Austrians, and their false reliance on their position, could, on the 1st of June, no longer be remedied, and nothing remained for them but to get quickly out of their false position, and withdraw behind the Ticino. They had been as completely outmanoeuvred as the Prussian

Novara—camp of the Chasseurs d'Afrique

PANORAMA FROM THE BRUGHIERE DI GALLIATE—THE PIEDMONTESE ARMY CROSSING THE TICINO

army was at Jena. There was, however, this difference in their favour, that, unlike the Prussians, they became aware of their awkward situation, and made an effort to extricate themselves from it.

In order to mask their retreat, they sent forward a small body of troops in the direction of the main body of the French army. This was sufficient to cause an alarm at dawn, on the morning of the 2nd of June; but it did not deceive the allies, who had received information that the mass of the Austrian army was hastily recrossing the Ticino at Vigevano.

The question was now only whether they would be in time to take up a position behind the Ticino, so as to offer battle to the allies, and to dispute their further advance. It was from that moment a trial of speed between the two armies. As for opposing the passage of the Ticino itself, it was too late; for, thanks to the success of the flank movement of the allies, they were nearer to the river than their adversaries; but behind the river, there is the Naviglio Grande, a canal constructed for the irrigation of the low lands of the Ticino. It issues from the river at Casa delle Camere, opposite Oleggio, and runs parallel to the river, at a distance varying from half a mile to four miles, until it reaches Abbiate-Grasso, where it makes a sudden turn in the direction of Milan. This canal is intersected by the main road from Novara to Milan, thus offering a position for the defence of that capital. To reach this point of intersection, which is at Ponte Nuovo di Magenta, and there to concentrate all available strength, became the task of both armies.

The importance of time was fully understood by the allies, for without losing one moment, they took their measures for the passage of the Ticino. Although there was every reason for supposing that the enemy was recrossing the Ticino, there was no reliable information to that effect on the 2nd of June, it was therefore thought dangerous to push on, without taking every precaution against a possible attack by the Austrians on the right bank. To guard against this possibility, it was determined to leave in position the four French *corps d'armée*, which, massed before Novara, were making front against the Austrians, and to employ the Garde Impériale to gain the passage over the river.

There are two passages over the Ticino, in the neighbourhood of Novara—that of Buffalora, and that of Turbigo. The first is the principal one, and over it runs the main road from Novara to Milan. A magnificent bridge, of huge granite blocks, constructed in 1810, by the French, connects the two banks of the river. So solid is its construction, and so roomy are its proportions, that it was intended to take over it the railway between the two countries,—an intention which has been carried into effect since the allies have taken possession of Lombardy. This is the bridge of Buffalora.

The other passage is that of Turbigo. It is from 5 to 6 miles higher up the river, and serves us an auxiliary means of communication between the two sides of the Ticino. Although tolerably frequented in the time of the Austrians, and provided with the inevitable passport and custom-house offices, it could only boast of a ferry-boat; the intention being to discourage, as much as possible, the intercourse between Sardinia and Lombardy, and to restrict it to a few main arteries of communication.

It was between these two passages that the allies had to choose, for they were the only points on the river, in the neighbourhood of their position, to which regular roads led, and consequently the only ones accessible to a large army.

The Ticino, like most of the feeders of the Po, is skirted on both sides by a plateau, which, according to the capricious windings of the stream, approaches and recedes, leaving sometimes only a narrow space between it and the river, and at other places a distance of a couple of miles. This plateau evidently indicates the old bed of the river, through which the waters have gradually eaten their way. Both at Ponte di Buffalora and Ponte di Turbigo, the river approaches close to the plateau on the right bank. Owing to the action of the stream, this latter has been worn away, and shows a bold precipitous line towards the river, which runs 40 to 70 feet below it. On the left bank, on the contrary, the plateau is at some distance from the river, leaving a space of more than a mile, which, by means of irrigation, has been converted into a rich plain covered with crops and trees. The right bank thus completely commands the left, which latter is therefore not defensible.

The Austrians, well aware of this circumstance, and yet anxious to have a *point d'appui*, partly for the defence of the river, partly to secure a retreat in case of need, constructed a *tête de pont* on the right bank at San Martino, on the road to the Ponte di Buffalora.

Coming from Novara, this road passes through a well-cultivated district abounding in crops of every kind, especially Indian corn, and studded with mulberry and willow trees. This lasts as far as the village of Trecate, which is just half-way from Novara to the Ticino. Soon after leaving Trecate, the aspect of the country changes; the signs of cultivation disappear, and an open, heathy country, with here and there a solitary tree, follows, through which the road runs in an almost straight line to the plateau overhanging the Ticino. Just at the edge of the plateau, overlooking the river, and commanding a magnificent view over the opposite bank, is a cluster of houses. This is San Martino, so called from an old inn of the same name. Besides this inn, there are the buildings which served formerly as the Sardinian customhouse and police-office, to which, in latter years, the railway station had been added: here was formerly the limit of the Sardinian territory, and the seat of the frontier authorities. Beyond San Martino the road descends abruptly towards the bridge, which is scarcely two hundred yards distant from it.

This, then, was the point chosen by the Austrians for a *tête de pont*. Evidently they attached great importance to the position, for no labour was spared to convert the approach to the Ticino into a formidable-looking intrenchment. Not only was the cluster of houses and the railway-station included, but likewise a solitary house, a quarter of a mile further north. The whole space thus closed in comprised an area of at least half a square mile, and all this ground was converted into a large horn-work, carried back on both flanks to the very edge of the plateau, and provided, according to all rules of the art, with a wide ditch, parapets, and embrasures for seventeen guns.

While so much care had been taken to guard the approaches to the Ponte di Buffalora, nothing was done by the Austrians to defend the passage at Turbigo except removing the ferry-boat, which served as the means of communication at that place. This circumstance alone would have been sufficient to point out the passage of Turbigo as the one to be preferred; not that the *tête de pont* at San Martino was very formidable; it looked more so than it was in reality; but, however weak, it was sufficient to allow a few thousand determined men to defend themselves for some time, even against superior forces, and thus gain time for the Austrian army to come up and take a position behind the Ticino, on the road to Milan. Besides this obvious reason for effecting a passage at Ponte di Turbigo, rather than at Ponte di Buffalora, there were two even more urgent grounds for this choice. The first of these was, that Ponte di Turbigo is six miles higher up the river, it was consequently so much further removed from the main body of the Austrians, which had to come up from Mortara and Vigevano; thus there was more chance of gaining the opposite bank before any large bodies of Austrian troops could be brought to oppose this passage. The second was that, by crossing at Turbigo, without delay, it was possible to gain not only the left bank of the river, but likewise the opposite bank of the Naviglio Grande Canal, and thus to overcome this formidable obstacle, and open the road to Milan. The canal is here only a mile and a quarter from the river, and its banks are less steep and precipitous than lower down—hence less calculated for defence.

Turbigo having been chosen as the point of passage, the division of the *voltigeurs* of the Garde Impériale, commanded by General Camou, received, in the afternoon of the 2nd of June, orders to proceed from Novara, through Galliate, to the Ponte di Turbigo, to protect the construction of three pontoon bridges. At the same time General Espinasse was ordered forward with one of his brigades to Trecate, on the road to the Ponte di Buffalora, to make a demonstration on that side.

The division of *voltigeurs* arrived at Ponte di Turbigo without meeting with any trace of the enemy and established itself on the banks of the Ticino. The pontoons being in readiness, the bridges were begun a little after nightfall, and completed by next morning, without any resistance worth that name on the part of the Austrians. The official account speaks of no resistance at all, while the pontonniers at the bridge told a story of sporadic bullets sent over by riflemen concealed in the woods, and Austrian lancers firing harmless pistol-shots.

As soon as the first bridge was ready, the first brigade of the *voltigeurs*, commanded by General Manèque, passed over to the opposite bank, and without stopping longer than was necessary to reconnoitre the thickly-wooded country on both sides, proceeded to the village of Turbigo. There is a gentle rise from the left bank, which lasts for little more than a mile, up to the point where the

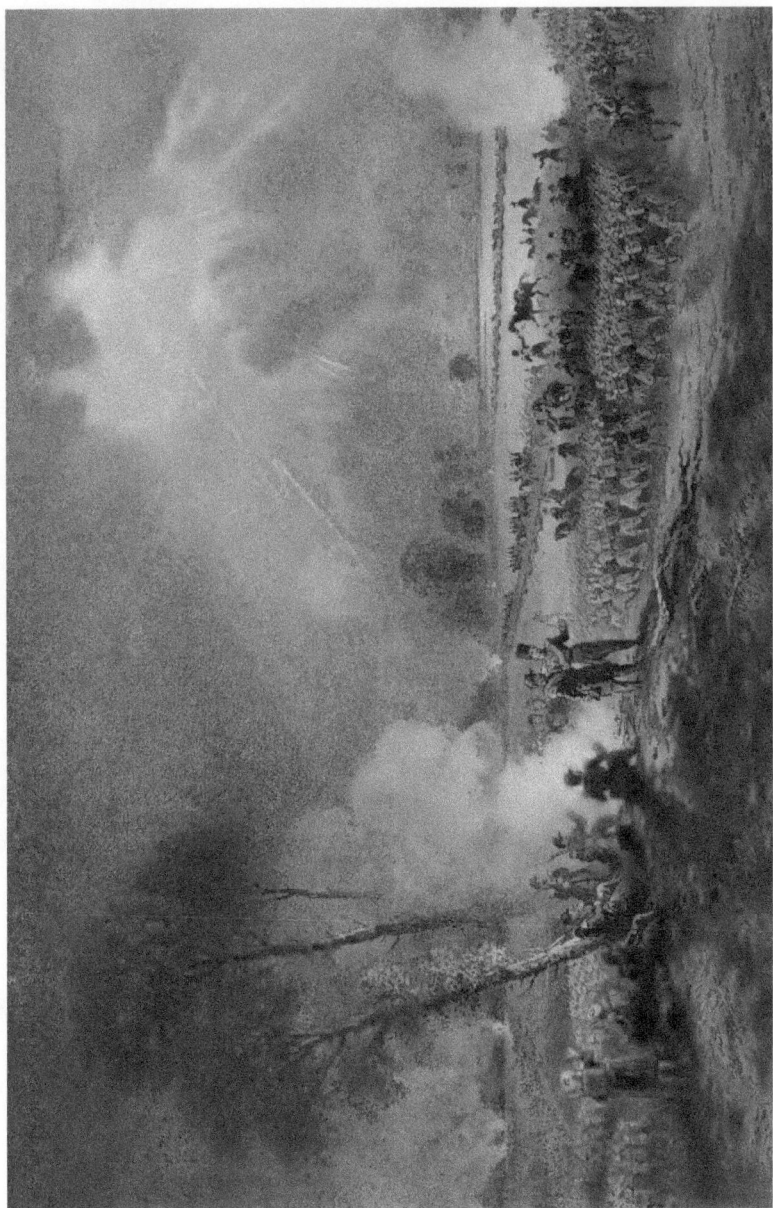

THE SECOND FRENCH CORPS (McMAHON) CROSSING THE TICINO AT TURBIGO

road crosses the Naviglio Grande Canal; immediately beyond the latter is a more abrupt rise, corresponding to the plateau on the right bank, but neither so high nor so steep. On its outskirts, is built the village of Turbigo. In this village, the brigade of the *voltigeurs* took up its position, observing the roads towards Castano and Cuggione. The second brigade remained on the right bank of the river, for the protection of the bridge. Thus, on the morning of the 3rd of June, the allies set their foot for the first time on Lombard soil.

While this was passing in the direction of Turbigo, General Espinasse advanced, as above mentioned, on the afternoon of the 2nd of June, with one brigade of his division, to Trecate, and showed himself in the direction of the *tête de pont* of Buffalora. This move, meant only as a demonstration, had the effect of inducing the Austrians to abandon the earthworks which they had so laboriously constructed at San Martino, and at five o'clock an explosion in that direction announced that they had blown up the bridge of Buffalora, and withdrawn to the left bank. Next morning at dawn, General Espinasse took possession of San Martino, where he found three howitzers, two field-pieces, and several ammunition-waggons; clearly showing that the Austrians had mistaken the demonstration for an attack, and in their hurry had left these trophies to their adversaries. A reconnaissance was pushed forward towards the bridge, when it was found that the Austrians had been unsuccessful in their attempt to blow it up. They had laid their mines in the second pier from the left bank, so as to bring down the two arches which it supported; the mine sprang, but it had not sufficient strength to destroy the arches. The top of the pier had given way, and the huge masses of granite, although somewhat disjointed, still reposed on its ruins; yet the gaps between the blocks looked so formidable, that at the first moment it seemed more than problematical whether it ever could be used. A report on this state of things was immediately despatched to the emperor, at Novara.

Although during the advance of the allies through the plain of the Sesia and the Lomellina, it had been invariably found that the Austrians covered the country with their field-works more for amusement than use, no one could be prepared for the evacuation of San Martino. According to the statement of an Austrian colonel of the staff, who was wounded and taken prisoner at the Battle of Magenta, this decision was taken because on inspection of the works, it was found that they had been so badly constructed as to be altogether untenable. To this statement, which the author himself heard, and to which, having examined the long and ill-flanked curtain of the earthwork, he fully subscribes, must be added the weakness inherent in field-works, with a defile behind them over which the retreat must be made. There is scarcely an example in the history of war, of such works being held successfully, for even the steadiest troops are more likely to think of their retreat than of the defence of their position. According to the statement of the same Austrian officer, the imperfect blowing-up of the bridge was owing to the want of blasting-powder. When General Clam-Gallas arrived in great haste for the defence of the Ticino line, this want was discovered, it seems, for the first time; he telegraphed to Milan, and the answer was returned, that there was no blasting-powder nearer than Verona. In consequence, the bridge of Buffalora was blown up imperfectly, and those over the Naviglio Grande not at all.

The evacuation of San Martino, and the blowing-up of the bridge of Buffalora, left little doubt of the intention of the Austrians to abandon the right bank altogether; but whatever uncertainty might have still remained, was removed by the arrival of King Victor Emmanuel, who reached Novara at eight o'clock in the morning of the 3rd, and brought the news that the Sardinian troops had found Robbio abandoned, as well as Mortara, and that the Austrians were in full retreat to the other side of the Ticino.

In the wake of the King followed the Piedmontese army, the division Cialdini, the victors of Palestro, forming the vanguard. After the outburst of joy which had met first the *corps d'armée* of General Niel, then the Garde Impériale, the emperor himself, and the king, one might have thought the enthusiasm of the good Novarese exhausted, as well as their store of flowers. Both seemed to have grown up afresh at the sight of the men of Palestro, and the old gloomy houses themselves seemed almost to smile, so bright and joyful was all around them as the division Cialdini passed on through the narrow streets towards Turbigo.

Three bridges over the Ticino being constructed at Turbigo, and no doubt now left about the retreat of the Austrians to the left bank, no time was lost in throwing a strong force on to that side of the river, and thus securing the passage for the rest of the army. The 2nd *corps d'armée* under General MacMahon, consisting of troops brought over from Africa, received orders to cross the Ticino on the pontoon bridges constructed the night before, and occupy the village of Turbigo on the opposite bank, in addition to the first brigade of the *voltigeurs* of the Imperial Guard, which had before gone there. The second brigade was likewise to follow, and then the whole Sardinian army, which was fast coming up from the Lomellina, and encamping on both sides of the road from Novara to Ponte di Turbigo.

The 2nd *corps d'armée* began its movement at half-past eight, on the morning of the third. General Espinasse, who, with one of his brigades, still occupied San Martino, left it, and joined the rest of his division by a cross road. That day and part of the next, during which this great movement of from 60,000 to 70,000 men, with all their baggage, lasted, the road from Novara to the Ticino, as well as the banks of the latter, offered a spectacle which can scarcely be imagined, much less described. This mass of human beings and quadrupeds all moved by one will, and in one direction, yet each trying to assert a certain amount of individual volition; this order in the general confusion; the variety of incidents breaking the uniformity of the march; the similarity of dress, yet diversity of costumes; the laughs, songs, shouts; the neighing, snorting, braying, above the general buzz of the multitude; the flash of the bayonets, and the multitude of colours flashing through the dense mass of white dust;—neither pen nor pencil can ever portray. And all this in a country made to set it off to the greatest advantage; the first half of the road up to the valley of Galliate, a complete contrast with the second half towards the Ticino; the first passing among rich cornfields, surrounded by a monotonous and melancholy line of willows, and intercepted by rows of stiff and uninteresting mulberry-trees, both sufficiently close to spoil the views of the Alps; the second leading to an open heath, with few trees and brushwood, and behind them Monte Rosa and his followers, and a number of picturesque *companiles* of the villages on the other side of the Ticino. And then the view of the Ticino valley from Ponte di Turbigo, which is a picture in itself, and wants no setting off. It is not seen until one is on the very edge of the plateau, when the panorama opens out.[1] Looking down, the eye follows the windings of the white road through the thick brushwood to the river, which runs at the bottom of the valley in three branches. The two smaller ones having been canalized, the swamps have disappeared, and a rich mass of young oaks and chesnuts has taken their place, with now and then a corn-field, which sets off the woods by its golden hue. On the opposite side of the third and main stream a guard-house, used formerly as the Austrian customs and police office, looks through the foliage of the trees which thickly clothe the opposite bank of the river. These woods continue on the gradually-rising ground, until they mix with the verdure of the Alps, and the mass of green is relieved by the white houses and churches of the villages of Turbigo, Robbichetto, Cuggione, Buffalora, and Magenta, which lie almost in a line on the plateau which skirts the Ticino on the Lombard side. Whoever saw this picture animated with long caravans of soldiers, Turcos, Zouaves, infantry, cavalry, artillery, pontoons, waggons, carriages, mules, bat-horses, appearing and disappearing according to the windings of the road, will never forget the sight.

The first division of the second corps began to pass the bridge at half-past one; at the head of it the swarthy Turcos, in their light-blue dresses set off with yellow and white turbans. As soon as they had passed, a reconnaissance was pushed forward towards Robbichetto, which is a mile and a half from Turbigo, on the road to Buffalora; and, like both these villages, situated on the verge of the plateau skirting the valley of the Ticino. There are two roads between, from Turbigo to Robbichetto, one leading to the southern, the other to the western portion of the village, while the road to Buffalora leaves the village in an easterly direction. Information having been received that Robbichetto was occupied by a body of Austrians who had arrived that morning from Milan, General de la Motterouge received orders to dislodge them. The disposition was as follows: the 1st battalion of Turcos formed in columns of divisions, and preceded by two companies of skir-

---

1. Mr. Bossoli's sketch gives an excellent idea of our side of the panorama, showing the villages of Turbigo, Robbichetto, the scene of the fight of the 3rd June between them, and, farther to the right, Cuggione and its castle.

THE BRIDGE OF——PARTIALLY DESTROYED, STILL AFFORDS A PASSAGE FOR INFANTRY

mishers, was to attack the village from the south side; the 3rd battalion, forming the left column, and similarly disposed, was to attack it from the west; the 2nd battalion was formed a little behind, *en échelon*, between the two, destined as a reserve to both. A battery of reserve artillery, under the personal command of General Auger, followed the regiment.

With this force, General de la Motterouge advanced at two o'clock in the afternoon, towards Robbichetto. The 45th regiment, which was the second of the first brigade, hastened its march over the bridge, and followed in the wake of the Turcos. At the same time, the 2nd brigade of the division de la Motterouge was directed towards the road to Castano, so as to flank the converging attack of the Turcos.

Arrived at the village, the column found the Austrians in position at the entrance of it, and was received by a brisk fire. The Turcos, without wasting many of their cartridges, gave one of their savage guttural Arab yells, and threw themselves, with the bayonet, on the Austrians, who, probably astounded by the novelty of the sight, did not hold for one instant. In a few minutes the village was cleared, and the Austrians were retreating on the road towards Buffalora, with the Turcos after them. In order to check the pursuit, the Austrians brought up some guns, which stopped the Turcos for one moment. The French artillery replied, and soon the rout of the Austrians was complete. Equally unsuccessful was a demonstration made by some Austrian cavalry, on the left from the direction of Castano. It was met by a battalion of the 65th of the line and two guns, and turned, after having received two shots from this latter. The enemy was pursued for some distance on the road to Buffalora, after which the column encamped on the battlefield.

The French loss was trifling, according to the official account,—1 officer killed, and 4 wounded; of soldiers, 7 killed, and 38 wounded; which is probably correct, as there was no resistance. If one had to judge of the Austrian loss by the number of arms, knapsacks, shakoes, bonnets, and other accoutrements, left on the battlefield, it must have been considerable. Of dead there were not a hundred; of prisoners none; of wounded very few. A field-piece had been left behind in the hurry. Thus ended what the official report calls "the combat of Turbigo." On the evening of the same day, the whole

2nd *corps d'armée* and the rest of the division of the *voltigeurs* of the Garde Impériale had passed the Ticino.

While this was passing at Turbigo and Robbichetto, the emperor himself went down in the afternoon to San Martino, and had the bridge of Buffalora examined. It was found that, although somewhat disjointed, it was strong enough, not only to carry infantry, but likewise cavalry and artillery, provided the gaps between the blocks on the surface were bridged over with beams and planks. This being ascertained, it was determined to take definite possession of the left bank of the Ticino the next day.

CHAPTER 5

The Battle of Magenta

From the information received, it was to be gathered that the Austrians had some troops at the Ponte Nuovo di Magenta, the point where the high road and the railway to Milan are intersected by the canal; but it was by no means clear that they intended to bring up the main body of their army from Vigevano, and make a stand on the road to Milan. On the contrary, it was probable that they would not have sufficient forces to risk a battle there; for their retrograde movement began only in the night of the 2nd of June, and there are 24 miles from Mortara to Magenta, by Vigevano. Besides this, the position on the canal was strategically turned by the column at Turbigo, and consequently untenable. This must be kept in mind, in order to understand many things in the battle of the 4th of June, which otherwise would be inexplicable.

The dispositions for the day were:—The 2nd corps (of General MacMahon) reinforced by the *voltigeurs* of the guard, and followed by the whole Sardinian army, was to march from Turbigo on Buffalora and Magenta, while the division of the grenadiers of the guard was to pass over the bridge of Buffalora, on towards the canal, and thence to Magenta, followed by the 3rd *corps d'armée* of Marshal Canrobert. The first column, which had already turned the position on the canal, was the principal one, and the second merely to make a diversion.

This disposition, although strategically, quite correct, shows at once that no general battle was expected; for the two remaining French *corps d'armée*, the 1st and 4th, were altogether left out of the combination,—the 1st corps being left where it was

THE TICINO

at

THE BRIDGE OF BUFFALORA & TURBIGO

and

THE BATTLE FIELD

of

MAGENTA.

encamped, before Novara, and the 4th only moved forward to Trecate; nay, even the 3rd corps, which was to act as a reserve to the grenadiers of the guard, only started from Novara on the morning of the fourth.

About ten o'clock, the emperor, accompanied by his staff, left Novara in an open carriage for San Martino, to direct himself the operations on that side. After the withdrawal of General Espinasse from the *tête de pont* at San Martino on the morning of the 3rd, it had been left unoccupied, and on the morning of the 4th the division of the grenadiers of the guard was still encamped at Trecate.

Its 2nd brigade, commanded by General Wimpfen, which was to lead the way, began its movement at eight in the morning. It arrived at the bridge of Buffalora about ten, and some beams and planks being laid over the damaged part of the bridge, it crossed and established itself on the opposite bank, without meeting anything, except some outposts of the enemy, who withdrew at its approach. As soon as this was done, a pontoon bridge was begun, a little above the stone bridge.

At ten o'clock the 1st brigade of the grenadiers, commanded by General Cler, two squadrons of *chasseurs* of the guard, under General Cassaignolles, three batteries of field and two batteries of horse artillery, the whole under the command of General Mellinet, followed the brigade Wimpfen, and arrived at Ponte di Buffalora at half past eleven o'clock.

In the mean time, the brigade Wimpfen, which had crossed the river, finding no resistance, and the enemy's few outposts retreating, advanced on the high road and through the fields on both sides of it, towards the Ponte Nuovo di Magenta, exchanging shots with Austrian riflemen, and the couple of guns which the Austrians had shown. This desultory fight, which originated in a desire for distinction, lasted till one o'clock, when the Austrians had retired to their position at Ponte Nuovo di Magenta, and the order came to stop the advance, and draw back nearer to the bridge of Buffalora.

As the principal attack was to be made from Turbigo, against the flank of the position, it was natural to avoid a hasty attack in front before the flank movement had begun to tell, and up to one o'clock there was no sign of this. A good deal of anxiety was felt on account of this delay, by which a considerable part of the day was lost, and the cause of which could not be ascertained, the two columns of attack being separated by the Ticino, and having no nearer line of communication than by Turbigo.

At last, about two p.m., the sound of cannon in the direction of the village of Buffalora announced that the turning column of General MacMahon had reached the battlefield and engaged the enemy. This was the signal expected for making the diversion from Ponte di Buffalora, by which the attention and forces of the enemy were to be divided.

In order to understand this diversion, and the whole battle, it is necessary to say something of the nature of the ground, and the dispositions of the Austrians. The plateau.[1] which skirts the Ticino on its left bank, runs from Turbigo down to Buffalora parallel to the course of the river. At this latter place the ridge makes a sweep away from the river, for a quarter of a mile, when it again resumes its original direction. In this it continues for about a mile and a half, and then throws out a spur towards the river, behind which lies the village of Ponte Vecchio. Thus from Buffalora to Ponte Vecchio a semicircle of positions is formed, or rather a long curtain, flanked by two bastions, facing the river, and about a mile and a quarter in length. The Naviglio Grande Canal, which from Turbigo to Buffalora runs at the foot of the ridge, penetrates the latter at the village of Buffalora, and keeps 100 to 150 yards behind it all along this position. The breadth of the ridge is nowhere more than 200 yards, and beyond it begins the Lombard plain corresponding to the plain of Novara.

A mile and a half in the rear of the ridge lies the village of Magenta. At the latter point converge all the roads coming from that part of the Ticino, and unite with the main road which runs to Milan. The Austrians could not very well overlook the importance of this point, for if it fell into the hands of the enemy, they were cut off from the straight road to Milan. Surprised by the appearance of the allies on the Ticino, they had been ever since the 2nd trying to concentrate and bring up their army, dispersed in the Lomellina and on the Po. But the distance was too great;

---

1. Mr. Bossoli's sketch is taken from the Lombard side of the Ticino, and shows off well the wooded plateau which skills the opposite banks, as well as the position of San Martino, where the Austrians had made their *tête de pont* towards the plain of Novara.

FIGHT IN THE VILLAGE OF BUFFALORA

and on the morning of the 3rd the *avant-garde* had scarcely passed beyond Abbiate Grasso. In this predicament nothing remained to oppose to the allies on the Ticino in the first instance, but a part of the 1st Austrian corps, under General Clam-Gallas, which had lately arrived from Bohemia, and was waiting for the rest of the corps in Milan and its neighbourhood. What portion of it had arrived, and what was its strength, will very likely never be known, for it is in the interest of the Austrians to diminish, and in that of the French to increase it; however, if we consider the extent of the positions held by the Austrians at noon, when, according to their own account, only one division of the main body of their army had arrived, we cannot but suppose that the greater part of the infantry of the 1st corps, at any rate, had arrived—that is, from 20,000 to 25,000 men.

It was a portion of this which had been pushed forward the day before, towards Turbigo, and had made acquaintance with the Turcos. The combat of Turbigo cannot have left the smallest doubt in the mind of the Austrian commander at Magenta that he had to expect an attack on that side of his position, and the most natural disposition would have seemed to make front towards the road leading from Turbigo to the villages of Magenta and Buffalora. This seemed so much the more reasonable, as the mass of the Austrian army, from which alone he had to expect help, was coming up on the road from Abbiate Grasso to Magenta; that is, perpendicularly to such a line of battle. But there were circumstances which made the pure and simple adoption of this front impossible; there was, namely, the probability that the French would make likewise an attack from Ponte di Buffalora, and thus not only endanger his left flank, but likewise his junction with the main body of the Austrian army. This probability became a certainty on the morning of the 4th, when the brigade Wimpfen pushed forward in that direction long before the main attack from Turbigo began.

In this dilemma, he had recourse to one of the most extraordinary lines of battle which perhaps ever occurred in the history of warfare. He leant his left wing on Ponte Vecchio and on Robecco, where the road from Abbiate Grasso to Magenta crosses the Naviglio Grande Canal. From Robecco he extended his line along the ridge above described, as far as Buffalora, which became the centre of his position. From Buffalora he leant back his line along the road towards the village of Magenta, which thus became an *appui* for his right wing, and at the same time, as the most central point in the position, was chosen as a *place d'armes* for his reserves.[2]

A look on the map at the three points of Robecco, Buffalora, and Magenta, will show that they form almost a rectangular triangle, and that the first Austrian line of battle ran along the two longest sides of it, with an acute angle between them. In order to moderate the inconvenience naturally resulting from this disposition, two brigades were pushed forward, one from Buffalora to Casale, on the road to Turbigo, and the other to Marcello, on the road from Magenta to Turbigo. In this way it was hoped to retard the attack from Turbigo, which was the most threatening, because not protected by natural obstacles, until the main body of the Austrian army could come up during the day.

Such was the position, and such were the dispositions of the Austrians, when, at two p.m., the double attack of the allies began—from the Turbigo side by General MacMahon, and from the Ponte di Buffalora by the division of the grenadiers of the guard, under General Mellinet.

Between the bridge of Buffalora and the ridge occupied by the Austrians, there is a space of about a mile of low flat ground, evidently part of the bed of the Ticino formerly, but now canalized and rendered fertile by cultivation. It forms now a succession of corn and rice fields, the former of which were in full bloom on the 4th of June, while the latter were still under water. The fields themselves, like all fields in the plains of Upper Italy, are surrounded by rows of willows and poplars, closely planted, and are separated from each other by ditches several feet in width, used for irrigation. Through these lowlands two roads lead up to the ridge. Both start

---

2. Mr. Bossoli's sketch will help greatly the description of the battle-ground, for it will realize to the reader the distances as well as the nature of the ground better than any words or maps can do. In the foreground are the last two houses of Ponte Vecchio, with the Naviglio Canal between them. Beyond the railway, the Ponte Nuovo Bridge, with the houses on both sides of the Canal, the road to Magenta, and the village itself on its extreme right. la the background, finally, beginning from the right, are Marcello, Cuggione, Turbigo, Robbichetto, Buffalora just in the centre, and Galliate, San Martino, Novara, and Trecate to the left.

from the bridge of Buffalora; one is the great highroad to Milan, a large, well-kept *chaussée*, rising gently above the lowlands on both sides, until at its approach to the ridge it attains an elevation of 30 feet above them. It runs in a straight line, intersects the ridge, making a gap in it like a deep railway-cutting, crosses the canal over a stone bridge, and leaving the other side of the ridge, continues in a straight line to the village of Magenta. The point of intersection is called Ponte Nuovo di Magenta, in distinction to the Ponte Vecchio di Magenta, which crosses the canal at the village of that name, situated half a mile lower down, in the direction of Robecco.

The other road, which is the old road to Milan, starts from the bridge to the left of the present main road, and leading in a multitude of bends through the lowlands, crosses the ridge and canal just before entering the village of Buffalora; after leaving this village, it makes a sudden bend to the right, and goes in a straight line to the village of Magenta, uniting with the present main road a little before it reaches the village.

Besides these two roads, there is the railway embankment, which, starting likewise from the bridge, diverges a little to the right, so as to avoid the main road; it cuts through the ridge a few hundred yards lower down than the latter, and, after crossing the canal, makes a bend to the left, intersects the main road, and comes out to the north-west of the village of Magenta.

The grenadiers of the guard were formed in two columns. The left, composed of the 2nd regiment, under Colonel d'Alton, was directed by the old road on Buffalora, with orders to pass the canal and co-operate with the column which General MacMahon was to send against Buffalora. The right column, composed of the 3rd regiment of grenadiers, under Colonel Metman, was sent on the main road against the position of Ponte Nuovo di Magenta. The Zouaves de la Garde, under Colonel Guignard, who form part of the grenadier division, was to follow the 3rd regiment as support. On the road itself, a section of artillery (two pieces) was to keep pace with the Zouaves. The 1st regiment of Grenadiers was kept near the bridge as reserve.

The first column advanced on the narrow, ill-kept road, towards Buffalora, without meeting with any sign of the enemy until it approached the village itself. The village is built in two portions, separated by the canal, the far larger part of it being on the opposite or left bank of the canal. Either the Austrians never seriously intended to defend the portion of the village on the right bank of the canal, or else the soldiers knew that the bridge was mined, and everything ready to blow it up; at any rate, after a short struggle, and with the loss of a few men, the 2nd Grenadiers drove them back over the bridge. In coming up to the banks of the canal they were received by a smart fire from the opposite bank, which was well lined, not only with infantry and riflemen, but likewise with some guns defending the approach to the bridge. This gave just time enough to the Austrians to withdraw to the left bank and blow up the bridge, thus placing the canal, which is at least 30 feet wide, and 10.15 feet deep, between them and their assailants. The latter attempted to repair the damage, and two of the *commandants* of the regiment were killed while exposing themselves to the riflemen who were in position on the opposite bank; but the grenadiers could not effect their purpose, and a desultory firing from one shore to the other was kept up until the column of the corps of General MacMahon, arriving from Turbigo, drove the Austrians from the village.

While this was passing towards Buffalora, the 3rd regiment of grenadiers advanced on the main road towards Ponte Nuovo di Magenta, driving before them the few outposts which the enemy had sent out after the withdrawal of this regiment in the morning. But the column had not advanced half-way, when three guns opened their fire upon them, one taking them in the right flank from the point where the railway embankment cuts through the ridge, and two others which were brought up on to the main road. In order to avoid the fire of these guns, the 3rd regiment of grenadiers was ordered down into the fields between the main road and the railway embankment, while the Zouaves descended into the fields on the opposite or left side of the road, leaving the two guns to return and attract the fire of the enemy's guns. This was done with good success, for the Austrian guns soon retired behind the barricades which had been erected at the point where the roads cut through the ridge.

Across the fields and ditches, sometimes knee-deep in water, at others ankle-deep in mud, the 3rd regiment of Grenadiers

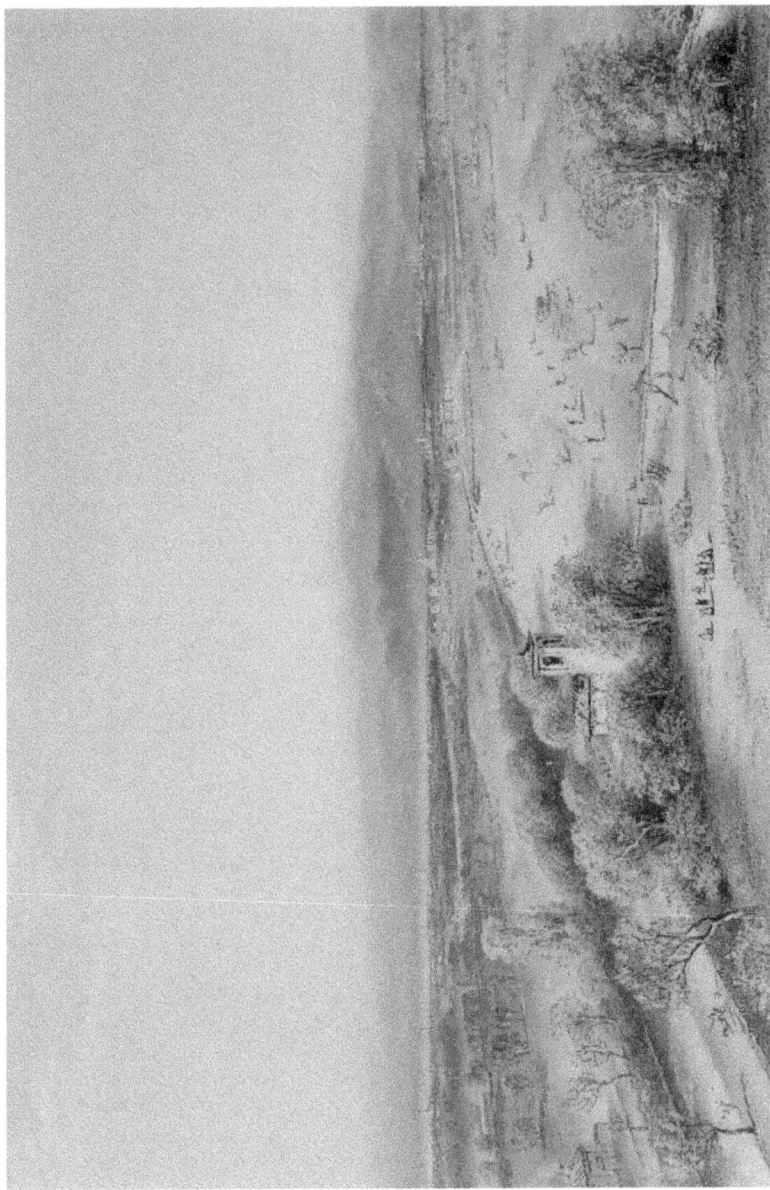

General view of the battlefield of Magenta

advanced towards the enemy's position, which only now, when looked upon from the low fields, appeared in all its strength. Rising suddenly to a height of fifty to sixty feet, the ridge looks more like a high artificial embankment than a natural formation. From Buffalora to Ponte Nuovo where the main road intersects it, it has been terraced and is planted with vines; from Ponte Nuovo to the railway embankment it is thickly planted with young trees, except just at the point where the embankment cuts through it; there it is bare. The Austrians had taken position on the top of the ridge along from Ponte Nuovo, to the railway embankment; but they were most thickly massed where the road and the railway embankment penetrate through the ridge. The entrance in both these places was strongly barricaded with beams, having only two embrasures in each for guns. They had made banquettes on the top, by throwing over the earth, and forming a parapet. The stuff requisite for the embankment, both of the road and of the railway, having been taken from the ridge, two cavities were formed inside, which were so regular that one would be almost inclined to think them made for defensive purposes; in these the Austrians had their reserves, which were thus under cover. The position was so good, that it seemed almost madness to attack it. The fields near the main road were too open to allow an attack from that point, without risking too much from flanking fire on both sides. Farther down, the trees planted on the sides of the ridge made an approach impossible. The least difficult point seemed that where the railway enters the ridge; this side was bare, and protected by the railway embankment against flanking fire from at least one side. And this point was chosen for the attack. The question was how to reach it, for at its foot was an unusually large open field, which had to be passed. The row of trees on the opposite end suggested the solution:—The 1st battalion of the regiment was formed behind it, and then made a rush over the open space. A hail of bullets showered down upon them as soon as the first men showed, and one of the guns posted behind the barricade on the railway embankment saluted them with grape; but before there was time to reload, the grenadiers, although rather thinned in numbers, were at the foot of the ridge. Here, without losing time in firing useless shots at their adversaries high above them, or without even waiting for a command, the knapsacks, and in many cases the bearskins too, were thrown on the ground, and a unanimous rush followed up the steep incline.

In less time than it takes to write down the deed, they had reached the top of the ridge, which had been as hastily abandoned by its defenders. The first grenadier who reached the top planted his bearskin on his musket; a hearty cheer of *Vive l'Empereur* from below answered, and the rest of the regiment scrambled up as fast as the loose ground, full of stones, permitted. The rush was so quick, that one of the guns which the Austrians had in position at the railway embankment was left behind. Without stopping longer than was necessary to collect the first battalions which had come up, the space from the edge of the ridge to the canal was traversed at a run, in chase of the Austrians, who were retreating precipitately over the bridge; over this now rushed friend and foe, leaping the gaps which remained between the iron plates of which the bridge is constructed, and out on the other side of the ridge, which the railway traverses under an arch made of bricks; nor did the *élan* stop there, but continued for a couple of hundred yards along the railway line and the vineyards on both sides of it. This headlong charge was dearly paid for, for as soon as the French ran out into the plain behind the ridge, they were received by a most formidable cross fire, which forced them to retire under the lee of the ridge.

The fact was, they had made a gap in the Austrian position, but by no means driven the Austrians away from it. They were still firmly established to the right and left at Ponte Vecchio and Ponte Nuovo di Magenta. In the former, they had established themselves in front of the detached houses, which, being mostly on a more elevated part of the ridge, overlooked the position near the railway bridge, and served as a *point d'appui* to the Austrians, although the buildings themselves were too far distant for an effective fire. At Ponte Nuovo di Magenta, on the contrary, they had occupied the buildings on the left bank of the canal, which served formerly as police and *douane* offices, as well as the two houses which are on the right bank of the canal. From the windows of these houses, several of which are built of granite, they opened a most galling fire on the column of grenadiers, at about 250 yards.

In order to avert this danger from both flanks, the two other battalions of the 3rd Grenadiers faced one to the right and the other to the left, and tried by their own fire to keep down that of the enemy. They were successful enough on the right at first, for by repeated attacks with the bayonet through the vineyards they made themselves a little room on that side. Not so on the left, where the houses of Ponte Nuovo were occupied by the Austrians, who, sheltered by the walls, were firing down as fast as they could load. It was soon clear that either the enemy must be driven from the houses, or the position abandoned. Accordingly, the 3rd battalion, which faced in that direction, received an order to take the houses; and under the command of Lieutenant-Colonel Tyron, they advanced along the ridge to the two houses which were on their (the Ticino) side of the canal. Even now, the bullet-marks on the walls show that taking them cost some trouble. The approach was mainly defended by the houses on the opposite banks of the canal, which were well lined with riflemen. By turning a little to the left, a part of the column at last got out of the range of this flank fire, and under the lee of the first house, which was then taken; this facilitated the taking of the other, which is only divided from it by the road leading to the bridge. In possession of both, a fusillade began between the 3rd battalion of grenadiers endeavouring to cross over the stone bridge, and the Austrians on the opposite side of the canal, which, however, led to nothing. The grenadiers could not take possession of this, as of the railway bridge; but the main road being now open to the bridge, the Zouaves de la Garde, who had hitherto taken no part in the action, were called up. Long taunted by the other regiments of Zouaves, and nick-named *les Zouaves de Paris*, they were anxious to show that, although they were now living in "*in otio eum dignitate*," they had by no means degenerated since they left Africa. Besides this, they had at their head General Cler, commanding the 1st brigade of grenadiers, of which the Zouaves form part. This brilliant young officer had been himself one of their body, and had been promoted to the rank of general for his distinguished conduct in the Crimea. Forgetting the general, and carried away by his own recollections, he put himself at their head, and led them on to the charge over the bridge, which was taken at a run, as well as the house to the right, after leaving the bridge; but it cost the Zouaves their gallant leader, who fell with a bullet through his breast. The two houses on the opposite side of the road still held out, and all attempts to dislodge the enemy by musketry-fire resulted merely in marking the buildings on both sides of the road. After half an hour of this desultory fire, recourse was had to steel, and the broad sabre-bayonet soon effected what lead could not do.

With the occupation of this house, the road to and over the bridge at Ponte Nuovo was open, like that of the railway line; and the position on the ridge taken, with the exception of the spur on which lies the village of Ponte Vecchio. But on that side the enemy had not until then shown great energy, which is explained by the circumstance that he had not yet received strong reinforcements. The 2nd battalion of grenadiers sufficed to keep him in check, and the rest of the 3rd Grenadiers, as well as the regiment of Zouaves, emboldened by the comparatively easy success they had hitherto obtained, debouched in the plain towards the village of Magenta, and advanced, the first on the railway line, and the latter on the highroad. But they had not gone far before they found themselves surrounded by a circle of fire.

The vineyards with which the ground is covered were alive with Austrian riflemen, who had drawn down the branches so as to conceal themselves; and behind these riflemen, large columns of infantry bore down, threatening to cut them off from the canal bridges. They were the reserves which, the Austrians kept in readiness, and which were not required just at that moment against General MacMahon, who had suspended his attack. In this emergency the two guns in action were brought forward on the main road, and an attempt made to keep off the enemy by this means. The 11th Chasseurs de la Garde, which formed part of the column, threw themselves towards the left, in the direction of the road from Buffalora to Magenta, and, in spite of the trees and vines, attempted to charge the enemy; but they could only succeed for one moment, and the whole body had to make a precipitate retreat towards the ridge and the canal. It was at this time that both grenadiers and Zouaves experienced their greatest loss, and that the only rifled cannon taken during the whole campaign fell into the hands of the Austrians. Nay, for one moment

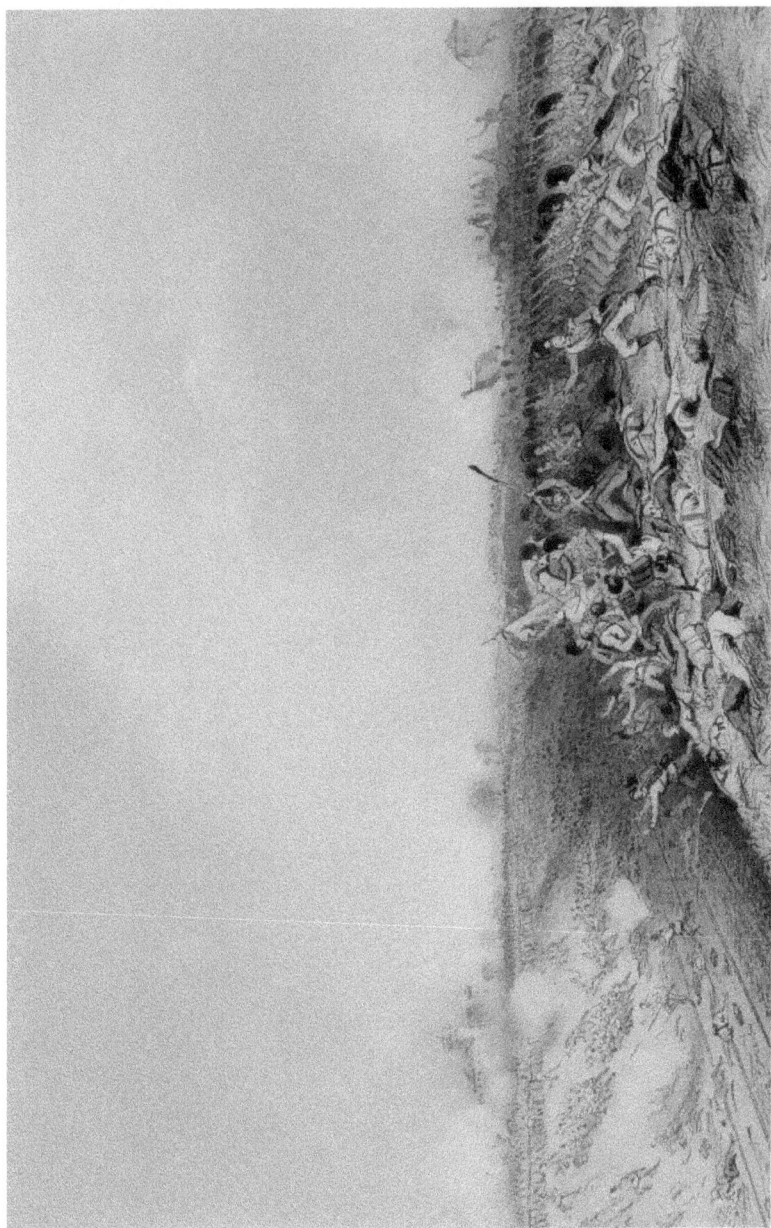

THE BATTLE OF MAGENTA

this hasty advance compromised even the position on the canal, and it was only after a great effort that the houses in front of the bridge at Ponte Nuovo, as well as the *débouché* over the railway bridge, could be occupied.

It was four o'clock in the afternoon. The position was by no means reassuring. The sound of battle had ceased on the left, where MacMahon was, which could not but suggest the idea that his attack had failed. This seemed the more probable, as the strong masses of reserves which the enemy mustered to retake his former position, indicated that there was no necessity for them elsewhere. At the same time he likewise began a strong offensive movement from Ponte Vecchio, which left no doubt that the mass of his army was beginning to arrive on the battlefield. The 3rd French corps, on the contrary, which had only left Novara the same morning, and was to have been by that time at Ponte Nuovo, to act as reserve to the grenadiers, as yet showed no sign of its appearance. It was the crisis of the battle, and an anxious time for the emperor of the French; *aide-de-camp* after *aide-de-camp* was sent on the road from Novara to hasten the march of the 3rd corps, while others were sent to Trecate to order up the 4th corps of General Niel.

Ignorant of what had happened to the main column of attack from Turbigo, it was all-important to retain the position on the canal, so as to be victorious at least on one point, if the attack had failed on the other. Besides, the position was absolutely necessary for debouching in the plain of Lombardy; and if it was lost, there was less chance of regaining it later in the day or the next day, as the enemy would, according to all probability, have brought up his whole army by that time.

How desperate the position seemed appears best from the circumstance that General Gyulai, who had then come up, telegraphed a victory to Vienna. The news, as our readers will remember, was transmitted by the wire to London, and caused the incredulity with which the French intelligence of a victory at Magenta was received the next day.

The 2nd grenadiers being still at Buffalora, the 1st regiment of this division remained alone as reserve. This was sent up as a reinforcement, with orders to hold the position to the last man. Here were three regiments, the 1st and 3rd grenadiers and the Zouaves de la Garde, originally not more than 4,500 men, and now certainly diminished by one-fifth, who had to stand the onset of the whole Austrian army, which by that time must have counted from 50,000 to 60,000 men. However brave, the little band could not have stood against them in the open field; but it was able to do so because of the favourable ground. Leaning their left on the houses in front of Ponte Nuovo, they occupied the reverse of the ridge towards the plain; although not so high as towards the Ticino, it still was a considerable advantage. Besides, the ridge being not more than 250 feet broad, they were sufficiently strong to repel any attack in their right flank from Ponte Vecchio.

Time after time the Austrian columns were led to the charge by their officers, and as many times they were repelled, leaving the ground strewed with their dead and wounded. For more than three quarters of an hour the three regiments fought this desperate battle. Fresh troops did the Austrians bring up at every onset, and every moment their numbers seemed to augment. Hopeless of taking the position in front, after so many efforts, they had thrown all their weight on its right flank, where it was overlapped by the projecting spur before Ponte Vecchio. It seemed only a question of numbers; but just when everything appeared most desperate, the brigade Picard of the 3rd corps was seen coming up *au pas de charge*. It consisted of the 8th Chasseurs, the 23rd and 90th of the line, and formed the vanguard of the 3rd corps. It had passed before the emperor at San Martino, and, encouraged by his words, had traversed the whole distance thence to the position at Ponte Nuovo, or more than a mile, at a run. It arrived *pêle-mêle*, and without waiting one instant to be formed, it rushed forward to the right of the position towards Ponte Vecchio to which the enemy was now quite close. Almost at the same moment the sound of cannon and musketry on the left front announced that General MacMahon had resumed the battle. To understand the panic which took place on that side, as well as the rest of the battle, we must now turn to the other half of the field, which henceforth plays the most prominent and decisive part. According to the dispositions of the previous day, the 2nd corps, composed of the divisions de la Motterouge and Espinasse, as well as the division of the Voltigeurs de la Garde, which had been placed under the orders of General MacMahon, left Turbigo at ten o'clock in the morning to march on Magenta. They were to be followed by the whole Sardinian army, which was to have formed the reserve for the left wing, and, if an opportunity offered itself, made a flanking movement on the right wing of the enemy.

The division de la Motterouge formed the right, and the division Espinasse the left column.

The first was directed from Turbigo, by Robbichetto, Malvaglio, Casati, and Buffalora, on Magenta, while the second took the road by Buscati, Inveruno, Mescro, and Marcello, towards the same point. The division of the *voltigeurs* was to follow the former of these two columns.

The Turcos were again the first to meet the enemy. They were at the head of the 1st division, and about noon found the enemy occupying Casati. They were ordered to clear the village, which was done with little trouble, as it contained mere outposts, too far distant from the main body to be supported with safety. After driving them from the village, the regiment took a position in front of it.

From the way in which the enemy had withdrawn from Casati, it was clear that he had some position in the neighbourhood to which he was falling back, and it was thought advisable to break the marching order and form in line of battle. This was likewise imperiously demanded by the nature of the ground. The road from Turbigo follows the plateau of the Ticinio, which is broader there than lower down towards Ponte Nuovo, and slopes almost imperceptibly towards the plain. The ground is full of vineyards, which are trained up trees, mostly ash, and all the fields are thickly planted with mulberry-trees, between which the crops are sown. The result of this is that the view is very much shut in, and affords considerable facilities for concealing bodies of troops. Besides this, there is a succession of large farmhouses, with many outbuildings, all surrounded by the same wall, and easily convertible into blockhouses.

Accordingly, the first division extending its right to the Cascina (farmhouse) Valizio, on the edge of the plateau towards the Ticino, and leaning its left on Cascina Malestella, formed in line of battle. Behind it, the *voltigeurs*, which formed its reserve, were massed in battalions at deploying distance. The enemy on his side was concentrating his forces in the direction of Buffalora and Cascina Gazza-

115

fama, which lies between Buffalora and Marcello, just where a cross road connects the two places.

The plan was to refuse the left, and force the enemy's position by the right at Buffalora, in order to effect a junction with the column which was coming from Ponte di Buffalora; but it could not be carried into effect before the left column arrived at Marcello, lest the enemy should throw himself between the two.

The road by which the division Espinasse marched, makes a great round, and is fully one-third longer than that by which the 1st division and the *voltigeurs* advanced. This seems to have been over- looked, for the latter, after forming its line of battle, had to wait an hour and a half before the division Espinasse reached Marcello. This was the primary cause of the delay of the corps MacMahon, which, it had been calculated, would be attacking Buffalora at one p.m., whereas it was past two o'clock before it could do so.

It was only at two p.m. that a report came from General Espinasse, that he had reached Marcello, and had the enemy before him. He was ordered to take the village, and then form his line of battle with his left at Marcello, and with his right in the direction of Cascina Gazzafama.

The official report of General MacMahon says:

As soon as I had acquired the certainty that these preparatory dispositions were completed, I made the division de la Motterouge, supported by the division Camou (Voltigeurs de la Garde), attack vigorously Buffalora.

But the fact is, that somehow or other, from that moment, something went wrong with the left column commanded by General Espinasse, which well-nigh lost, and certainly diminished the success of the day. What was the real cause can now only be conjectured, but will perhaps someday be brought to light by history.

As the reader will recollect, the Sardinian army was to have followed MacMahon's corps, and act as reserve to its left wing, formed by the division Espinasse, and it was only at seven p.m., when the battle was won, that the 2nd Sardinian division (Fanti) showed itself. The official bulletin published in the *Moniteur*, gives no key as to whose fault this was: it merely says:

The execution of this plan of operation was disturbed by some of those incidents which occur in warfare. The king's army was retarded in its passage over the Ticino, and only one division of it could follow, at some distance, the corps of General MacMahon. The march of the division Espinasse was likewise retarded.

From this, of course, nothing is to be gathered. As a faithful historian, the author must report that, both at headquarters and in the French army, that evening, as well as for some time afterwards, there was great indignation felt and expressed at the tardiness of the Sardinian army, which was supposed to be caused by offended vanity—that, in a word, the king thought it beneath his dignity to cross the Ticino in the wake of a French corps, and to place himself and his army under the command of a French general. All kinds of stories were circulated on the subject for several days, until, in the rapid march of events, the whole was forgotten. Thus, among the rest, a story was current of an interview the next day between the emperor and the king, in which all kinds of imaginary conversation were said to have been held, and high words exchanged between the two sovereigns. Whether true or not, it is a fact that in the French army and at headquarters, the tardy arrival of the Sardinian army was explained in this way. The impression was too general not to have some foundation, and be, as it were, the reflex of something coming from the emperor himself; but there are likewise facts, which, if they do not entirely remove the suspicion of something of the kind having occurred, still tend considerably to modify the general view taken of the matter by the French army at the time.

First and foremost among them is the fact, that daring the whole day the approach to the bridge was blocked up by waggons of the French train, following the corps which had passed the previous day They were mixed up with waggons and carriages belonging to the Sardinian army, of which several divisions, for example, the 4th of Cialdini, were still encamped on the Sardinian side of the Ticino. This fact receives additional weight, from the circumstance that the late arrival of the 3rd French corps on the scene of action is attributed by the emperor himself to the encumbrance of the road. We may, therefore, suppose that all was not right with the dispositions made for the march of the baggage.

Putting all these facts together, it seems obvious that it never was expected the mass of the Austrian army could be already at Magenta, and that a general battle was imminent; for, with such an expectation, it can scarcely be supposed that the baggage would have followed so close as to impede the movements of the troops. Besides this, it is quite possible that the commanders of the Sardinian army were not much inclined to play a subordinate part, and that the most was made of the encumbrance of the road, which was somebody else's fault. The country is nowhere so shut in as to prevent infantry marching across the fields, at least for some distance, nor can the whole road by Buscati to Marcello, on which the Sardinian army had to follow Espinasse, have been so encumbered by the baggage of one division as to render an advance on it an impossibility.

Finally, there seems to have been some delay on the part of Espinasse himself, which, however, only occurred in coming up to the position of Marcello. General MacMahon admits as much, when he says that "he sent General Espinasse word to hasten his movement on Mesero and Marcello;" unless, indeed, it be supposed that he was waiting for the appearance of the Sardinian army, and that the issuing of the order was merely not to retard his march any longer on that account.

These remarks are necessary, in order to understand the crisis of the battle which induced the Austrians to telegraph a premature victory to Vienna.

When the division de la Motterouge had formed its line of battle with the division of the *voltigeurs* in second line, the signal was given to advance on Buffalora. The Turcos and the 45th of the line, forming the first brigade, were on the right; and their task was to attack the position of Buffalora. This attack from the north was to be simultaneous with that of the 2nd grenadiers, who, as related above, attacked the position from the Ticino side. As the latter waited until the main attack began, the movement succeeded. The high road from Turbigo to Buffalora, before it reaches that place, descends from the plateau on which it runs, and, continuing for some time on lower ground, again ascends a few hundred yards

TAKING OF MAGENTA

from the village. It was on this road and in the fields on both sides of it that the Turcos advanced, while the 45th, to their left, went in the direction of the place where the cross road from Marcello runs into the Turbigo road.

The Austrians were found in position before the village, where they had thrown up some earthworks armed with guns and a rocket battery. Attacked from both sides, this outlying point could not hold out long, especially as the attack of the position at Ponte Nuovo likewise took place about the same time, which, if successful, might have endangered the troops encased in this angle of the position. After blowing up the bridge over the canal, so as to prevent au advance on their flank from that side, the position was abandoned, half by force and half by free will, for the question was to gain time until the reinforcements could come up, and to risk nothing.

As soon as Buffalora was taken, the line of battle was changed; the column made a quarter of a movement of conversion to the left, so as to lean its right on the road from Buffalora to Magenta, with its left in the direction of the Cascina Nuova, a large farmhouse situated near the road from Magenta to Buffalora. This was done with the view of effecting a junction with the left column before making an effort on the centre of the enemy at Magenta. This was so much the more necessary, as the enemy had strongly occupied another *cascina* called Gazzafama, which lies on the cross road from Marcello to Buffalora, and thus had taken up a position between the two columns.

The movement of conversion being executed, the *voltigeurs* of the Garde were placed to the left of Buffalora, and the column advanced. Resistance was first offered at Cascina Nuova, which was occupied by two regiments. It is one of those large farmhouses which occur all over Lombardy, built of stone, and it formed, as it were, an outlying post of the Austrian centre. It must be remembered that the Austrians were fighting against time, and felt that they had not, in the beginning of the battle, sufficient forces to be everywhere in strength. In order to diminish this disadvantage, they had concentrated all their reserves at Magenta, and occupied the two farm-houses of Cascina Nuova and Gazzafama, which are just in the middle between the two roads from Turbigo to Marcello, and from the same place to Buffalora; that is, the two roads on which it was probable that the enemy would advance. They had thus a chance of throwing themselves between the two columns, and were, at any rate, sure to force both to make an effort to gain these positions. The combination was the best which could be made under the circumstances, and if it did not succeed, that was not the fault of the commander.

The Cascina Nuova, which was the first of the two positions in front of the Austrian centre, was attacked by the 45th of the line. The Austrians were occupying not only the farm-buildings themselves, but likewise the ground about them, closely planted with trees and vineyards. The resistance was considerable in the beginning, owing to the extraordinary bravery of the Austrian officers, who exposed themselves to the utmost in order to keep the men up to the mark. Their efforts succeeded in arresting the progress of the 45th for some time; but many of the Austrian officers being killed or disabled, the resistance began to flag, and the *cascina* was taken. Fifteen hundred Hungarian troops laid down their arms, and the colours of one of the regiments were taken.

But while the 45th gained this success on the extreme right, the left column, which was to have united with the right at Cascina Gazzafama, made an unsuccessful attempt on the latter position. The Austrians, whose whole combination was based on preventing the union of the two, took advantage of this check, and threw themselves on the right flank of this column, pressing it back towards Marcello. It was here that the absence of the Sardinians began to tell, for the division Espinasse having no reserve, an effort made by the right column to relieve the pressure, and thus effect the junction, likewise failed. The Austrians, emboldened by success, now tried to throw their whole weight on this, the right column, and retake the Cascina Nuova. Afraid of the exposed position of his extreme right, which was thus far in advance of the rest, and seeing, likewise, no possibility of effecting a junction with Espinasse, MacMahon ordered the right column to retire.

It was a critical moment, not only for the corps of General MacMahon, but likewise for the rest ot the troops engaged—the division of grenadiers fighting a battle of despair against the mass of the Austrian army, which was coming up just at that time, and the division Espinasse cut off from the rest of the troops under

MacMahon's command. However, General MacMahon lost neither head nor courage. Instead of persisting in his original plan, he changed it according to circumstances. Finding that he could not effect his junction with Espinasse at Gazzafama, he determined to give up the idea, and make an effort with both divisions on Magenta itself, the enemy's centre. The division de la Motterouge, having the *voltigeurs* as reserve, was to form the main attack, so as to relieve the pressure from the others. The *voltigeurs* of the Garde were ordered up to form a second line *en échelon,* in the left rear of the division de la Motterouge, and the steeple of Magenta was given as a point of direction to the troops. All these dispositions took about an hour.

This was the pause, from four to five o'clock, which might have cost the French the victory, had it not been for the bravery of the grenadiers and Zouaves of the Garde and the mistakes of the Austrians. They naively thought themselves victorious on the side where MacMahon attacked, and in their confidence not only telegraphed a victory, but, what was of more consequence, they extended their line too far in front, and sent many of their reserves to take the position held by the grenadiers, thus weakening their position at Magenta.

A little before five, just when the reinforcements came up to the rescue of the grenadiers, General MacMahon resumed the offensive. The Austrians then occupied the railway line from the point where it intersects the main road to Milan; they held the station-house in force, having lined its windows with their riflemen, as well as the first houses which lie close behind, and the *campanile* of one of the churches. At the point where the road from Buffalora enters the village, they had a strong battery of artillery.

The 45th regiment which was now on the extreme right of the division de la Motterouge, received orders to march straight on the village, while General Auger, taking up a position to the right of the 45th, replied vigorously to the guns of the enemy in position in front of Magenta. It was then that the Austrians saw the mistake they had committed in sending off their reserves. They were now recalled, but it was too late; for while the 45th penetrated the village by the road of Buffalora, the *voltigeurs* of the Garde attacked the railway line, and took it with little sacrifice of men, before the Austrians could bring back their troops from the position on the canal. All they could do was to throw themselves into the houses of the village, and fight the battle of despair. Every house thus became a castle, held by a desperate garrison, which it required a regular combat to take. Volumes could be written on the incidents in which these combats abounded. An incredible number of officers being killed and disabled, the soldiers were left entirely to themselves in these isolated positions, from which there was no retreat. They had been told that they had to expect no mercy, as it was the habit of the allies to kill their prisoners and wounded; so they fought with an imaginary halter round their necks. The strongest of these fortresses was perhaps the cemetery behind the village. It fell to the share of the division Espinasse, which, while the division de la Motterouge attacked the village from the Buffalora road, made a converging movement on the village from the Marcello road, and attacked it on that side. It was while heading this assault that General Espinasse and his *aide-de-camp* were killed, almost at the same moment. By seven o'clock, the Austrians felt that they could no longer hold the position of Magenta, and they concentrated all their forces not cut off or shut up in the village to make their retreat towards Robecco and Corbetta, which were the two lines open to them. One of their columns, probably mistaking the road, retired on the main road towards Ponte Nuovo, and was taken in flank by the French artillery posted on the road from Buffalora, which is almost parallel to it. At the same time it was attacked in front by the division Vinoy, of the 4th corps, which had debouched from the position on the canal. Their retreat was changed into a complete *débandade*.

The two hours from five to seven p.m. which decided the victory of the French at the village of Magenta, were not lost on the other side. As related above, at the time that MacMahon resumed the offensive, the grenadiers, almost exhausted by their resistance, received the first assistance from the brigade Picard of the 3rd corps, which restored somewhat like equilibrium between the hard-pressed grenadiers and the continually-increasing forces which the enemy brought up from Ponte Vecchio. The fact was, that the mass of the Austrian army was now fast arriving, and concentrating at Robecco, Castellazzo dei Barzi, and Ponte Vecchio, with the evident intention of regaining at any price the position on the canal held by the grenadiers. As the Austrians thought themselves already victorious on the Magenta side, they not only made no efforts to strengthen it, but, as has been said, actually sent their reserves from Magenta against the grenadiers and Zouaves de la Garde; while these reserves made an effort against the front of the position, the troops which were arriving were employed to operate from Ponte Vecchio and the spur of the ridge running out towards the Ticino, on the flank and towards the rear of this forlorn hope.

The timely assistance of the brigade Picard became invaluable under these circumstances, as it enabled the French to make an offensive return towards the part of the village of Ponte Vecchio which lies on the Ticino side of the canal. It was so vigorous, that, in spite of the advantage afforded by the detached houses of which the village is composed, the Austrians were for a moment dislodged from it; however, having their whole army behind, they were soon able to bring up fresh troops, and drive back the French to their old position near the railway embankment. Just when the Austrians had thus again asserted their superiority, the division Vinoy of the 4th corps, which had been sent for by the emperor from Trecate, came up *au pas de charge* like the brigade Picard. General Niel, commanding the 4th corps, arrived with them.

This new reinforcement of from 7,000 to 8,000 men, increased not only the material strength, but also the moral confidence of the troops; for it was a sign that more reinforcements were at hand. As soon as the division had come up, the offensive was again re-sumed, on a larger scale. The enemy's reserves being concentrated at Robecco and Castellazzo dei Barzi on both sides of the canal, and his line similarly disposed on either bank at Ponte Vecchio, the division Vinoy debouched by the railway bridge to make an effort on the left bank of the canal, while the brigade Picard and the grenadiers again advanced against the part of the village situated on the right bank. At the same time, the artillery of the grenadier divisions was brought up to the ridge, and directed its fire on the reserves of the enemy. It was a regular Inkerman fight, each bat-talion for itself, or together with others, opposing the reserves of the enemy, which were all round them, advancing and retreating, making gaps, and having to fight their way back again. In this way both sides of the village of Ponte Vecchio were taken and retaken. The offensive return of the Austrians was facilitated by their having blown up the canal bridge at Ponte Vecchio, and thus isolated the two columns of the French, which were exerting themselves to keep possession of both sides of the village.

While this hand-to-hand fight was still undecided, Marshal Canrobert arrived about six p.m., with the brigade Janin, which, like the brigade Picard, belonged to the division Renault, the first of the 3rd corps. On his way to the battlefield, he occupied with a few companies the spur of the ridge that has been so frequently mentioned, and which, stretching out towards the Ticino, might have invited the Austrians to send a strong body clown to the low ground, and thus cut off the troops fighting on the plateau from the bridge and the reinforcements crowding over it. That being done, the brigade passed the canal near the railway, and took up its position beside the other troops at Ponte Vecchio. This was at seven p.m., just as MacMahon had succeeded in breaking the Austrians at the village of Magenta. It put an end to the fight on the canal side likewise. The fury of the combat was broken, and the French remained on the defensive in possession of Ponte Vecchio. The division Trochu of the 3rd corps, which arrived at eight, contributed to insure this possession. In the village of Magenta, the partial combats in the houses were prolonged until late at night; but the battle was won, and General MacMahon, Duc de Magenta and Maréchal de France, was the hero.

The French troops encamped on the ground which they had taken during the day; the 2nd corps and the *voltigeurs* in and about Magenta and Buffalora; the grenadiers, Zouaves de la Garde, and the brigade Picard, side by side on the bloody field, which the first had so gallantly taken, and both so bravely defended; the rest of the 2nd corps and the division Vinoy of the 4th corps at Ponte Vecchio, and in advance of it towards Robecco. Thus every inch of ground which the Austrians had occupied was in the hands of the French.

The emperor, who had remained the whole day at San Martino, to direct the operations and the bringing-up of the reserves, did not return to Novara, where all his household still remained, but passed the night on the spot which he had occupied during the day.

The trophies were four guns, one taken by the grenadiers, and

TAKING THE CEMETERY OF MAGENTA

three by MacMahon, two stand of colours, and 7,000 to 8,000 prisoners; and the results, the opening of the road to Milan and the evacuation of that capital by the Austrians.

These results were so clear that the reports of the Austrian generals, of undecided battle, intentions of renewing the attack on the next morning, as well as the insinuations of the emperor having been obliged to retrace his steps to Trecate, and all the other contrivances usually resorted to by defeated armies, were soon judged at their real value. Even those most disposed to take a charitable view of the matter, could scarcely keep up their illusions when they saw the Austrians evacuate Lombardy, and retire to the Mincio without risking another battle, except the fight at Melegnano to protect their retreat.

The loss on both sides was heavy, which could not be otherwise, considering the various fortunes of the day, and the obstinacy of the fight on some points. On both sides single regiments suffered disproportional loss, because they had to defend themselves against far superior forces. Thus, for instance, of the French, the 3rd grenadiers, the Zouaves de la Garde, the regiments of the brigade Picard, the 65th of the line, and the 2nd regiment of the Foreign Legion belonging to the 2nd corps, and the 85th of the 4th corps, were more than decimated, while other regiments suffered scarcely any loss; the same was the case with the Austrians, above all with the regiments which were there from the beginning of the day. Some of them were almost annihilated. The reader must not expect exact returns of dead, wounded, and missing, such as he is accustomed to see published in the British army. He will, probably, be aware that this is not the habit in continental armies. All, therefore, that can be given in this respect must be guess-work, gathered by walks over the battle-field, looking in at hospitals, talking to prisoners, and other such vague sources of information.

From these one would be justified in putting the French loss at 7,000 to 8,000 men *hors de combat*; while the Austrians, if they had had time next day for a roll-call, might have found themselves short of 18,000 men: among them were, no doubt, some who had been scattered, and found their way back afterwards; but, considering that they lost 7,000 prisoners alone, this cannot be far from the mark.

Comparing this loss with the whole number of men actually

engaged, it will be found smaller than might have been expected. The French had, in all, seven divisions on the spot. Although the regiments, with the exception of the two African divisions of Mac-Mahon, had not yet received the men who were on *congé renouvelable*, we may still assume the division at 8,000 men, which would make 58,000 men, of which they had lost one-eighth.

Among the Austrian prisoners and wounded were men belonging to the four *corps d'armée*, the 1st (Clam-Gallas), the 2nd (Lichtenstein), the 3rd (Schwartzenberg), and the 7th (Zobel); consequently it may be assumed that these four corps were on or near the battlefield, and available, even if the Austrians did not choose, or did not know how to employ them. The Austrian corps, during the war, consisted of from four to seven brigades, each on an average of 5,000 men. Taking a mean of five brigades only, the Austrians had about 00,000 to 100,000 present; their loss was, therefore, less than one-fifth.

If we compare, however, the losses with the men who actually took part in the fight, the proportion will be far greater. This is explained by the circumstance, that on neither side were the forces on the spot, but they came up by degrees, so that at one moment one, and at another the other, side had the advantage.

As was explained above, it was a race between the two combatants, who should come up the sooner, and get possession of Magenta, the key of the road to Milan. Yet, strangely enough, when it came to the point, neither used the efforts which might have been expected. From what precedes it may be gathered that either the allies did not expect to meet the mass of the Austrian army, or else made dispositions by which more than half of their army could not take part in the engagement. The former conjecture is by far the more probable, although, if this was the case, it is difficult to understand why they began their movements so late, as every moment was precious. If, for instance, the troops at Turbigo had begun their movement at four a.m., instead of eight, and the others similarly, they might have expected, with far more probability, to take the positions before the *gros* of the Austrian army could come up. As it was, it must not be forgotten that it was the first battle in which the emperor commanded, and it would have been too much to expect that no mistakes should be made by a man who makes his *début* in generalship with an army of from 130,000 to 150,000 men.

If, nevertheless, the result was a victory, it was owing to the soundness of the plan, the bravery of the troops, and the colossal blunders of the Austrians. As to the first of these causes, it put beyond a doubt the strategical capacities of the mind which conceived it; and had the execution corresponded, the emperor would have gained at Magenta the prestige which the Battle of Solferino gave him three weeks later. As to the bravery of the troops, it must be remembered that the French army had only left the neighbourhood of Alessandria six or seven days before, and had, without the smallest check, advanced in its victorious course, seeing the enemy retiring out of reach all the while. All were burning with the desire to measure themselves with the Austrians, and the retreat and escape of the enemy excited a feeling of disappointment in every French soldier. On the only two occasions, in which, during the campaign, the Austrians stood, a comparatively easy victory was gained over them. All this, taken together, created a great feeling of confidence in the troops, and a consciousness of superiority, which is of the greatest moment in the battlefield. The very reverse was the case with the Austrians; the sudden retreat could not but exercise a demoralizing influence, especially, as in the hasty march no disposition could be made to provide properly for the wants of the soldier. Most of those belonging to the main body of the army arrived hungry, weary, and faint. Even the rude instinct of the soldier descried that a gross blunder had been committed, and this must have considerably shaken his confidence. Last, but not least, so early as at the battle of Magenta, symptoms were apparent of what afterwards became so plain, namely, that the greater part of the Austrian soldiers had no heart in the fight. There was a kind of return of the killed and wounded published by the Austrian government, in which everyone could see the great proportion borne by the officers. The Austrian officers are dressed like the men, so there can be no other explanation than that they had to expose themselves more than usual, in order to make the men fight.

But quite as much is ascribable to the third, as to the two first causes,—namely, to the blunders of the Austrian commanders. The reader will remember a correspondence inserted in the *Times* a few months ago: one correspondent relating that the officer sent by Clam-Gallas in the morning to Gyulai, to ask for reinforcements, was detained to dinner, and that it was only after dinner that the order for marching was given to the troops at Abbiate Grasso; while the other correspondent maintained that he was with General Gyulai, who was himself on the battlefield by noon, or a little after. According to another account, it was General Hess who gave an order to halt the troops, which were already in march towards Magenta. Between all these contradictory statements, it is impossible for anyone who was on the other side to determine whether any troops, and what part of them, could have been on the battlefield in time; he can only relate the fact, that almost all the reserves of the Austrians came up by degrees, while the battle lasted, and that while it was raging most furiously, about five p.m., large masses of troops were collected at Robecco and at Castelazzo de' Barzi, which took no part in the action.

The mass of the Austrian army either could or could not be brought up in time. If it could, it was the commander's fault that it was not; if it could not, it was the commander's fault to accept a battle under such conditions. As it was, the main body was brought up just at the moment when it was too late, which leads us to the conclusion that the Austrian general, as many other Austrian commanders before him, never knew clearly what he was going to do, until he saw that nothing remained but to withdraw. The disposition of General Clam-Gallas in the beginning was probably the best that could be made under the circumstances, and his plan of occupying a position between the two roads on which the French army was likely to come from Turbigo, might possibly have succeeded, had he not been deceived by a momentary success on that point, pushed on too far, and sent off the reserves from Magenta, to attack the position of the grenadiers in front, by which he weakened his centre, and facilitated MacMahon's attack on it. Although both Gyulai and Hess were present, Clam-Gallas retained the command to the end of the day, and must, therefore, be made responsible for it.

In general, it appears from all circumstances, that the Austrian army was managed very much in a Bashi Bazuk manner, where everyone has something to say, and no one sufficient courage to take responsibility upon himself; of course Gyulai, being chief in command, must take the greatest share in the blame. The Austrians have a favourite anecdote in their army of the bold Prince Eugene of Savoy. When just on the point of giving battle to the Turks, he received a despatch from the Aulic Council of War, which directed the operations from Vienna. This despatch he put in his pocket unopened, gained the victory of Zenta, and on reading it afterwards, found that it contained strict orders not to meddle with the enemy. Tradition has preserved the anecdote, but there seemed no clanger of the Austrian generals acting in the Italian campaign according to the moral contained in it.

CHAPTER 6

From Magenta to Milan

Whoever saw the battlefield of Magenta on the morning of the 5th of June, will never forget the sight. It was the result of the first great shock between the two armies during the war, in comparison with which Montebello and Palestro were mere combats. Several square miles of carnage, well-nigh 2,000 dead and dying lying about, in some places in heaps, in others dotted all over the ground in every attitude; some with that placid countenance which indicates a well-aimed bullet in the heart or in the head, stiffened in the very position in which they were when the fatal lead struck them; here one with his right arm close to the hip, and with his fists clenched as if he was still holding the musket ready for the charge; there another, with his hand to his mouth and showing his white teeth, as if still ready to bite off the end of the cartridge; the next man as calm as though he were reposing; another near him with his features distorted, and his limbs cramped, exhibiting all the horrors of the death-struggle from a bayonet-wound; further on, one with his head off; another with his limbs shattered; a third reduced by a cannon-ball to a formless heap in a pool of blood; and so on, in all the endless varieties and forms of death. It was a study for an anatomist, or a gloomy painter of horrors.

And all around, mixed up with the dead were the wounded, some only just breathing, and too helpless to crawl under the shade of the next vine, or to chase away the flies feasting on the sweat of death; others cowering down in a ball, shivering under the scorching sun; others looking up imploringly and craving a mouthful of water; from one burst a sob, from another a sigh. It reminded one of Dante's "Inferno."

All the French and many of the Austrian wounded had been removed during the night, but on the third day after the battle, somewhere found lying about in the field, and brought in. This was owing in a great measure to the idea which had been inculcated in the Austrian soldier, that the allies ill-treated and killed the wounded; so they hid themselves, thinking the chances of starving preferable to certain death. Numbers concealed themselves in the cellars of the village of Magenta, and in the farmhouses near which they had been wounded.

All the points where the battle had raged most furiously, like Ponte Nuovo and Ponte Vecchio, the fields near the railroad, and the vicinity of the *cascine*, resembled the remains of a great rag fair; *shakoes*, knapsacks, muskets, shoes, cloaks, tunics, linen, all stained with blood, lying about in every direction, the soil trampled down, and ploughed up by cannon-balls; trees shattered, leaves with bullets through them; every inch of ground the scene of some drama of heroism and ferocity, or of some tragedy of war and misery.

And on this stage were now moving about numbers of soldiers of all arms, many of them actors in the scenes which had passed, others attracted by curiosity, and listening to the stories "of most disastrous chances, of moving accidents;" or examining dead and wounded with that morbid interest which on such occasions seems to benumb all feelings of humanity, and cover each heart with a triple armour of insensibility. Among the crowd the fatigue-parties worked cheerfully at their nauseous task of removing the wounded and burying the dead. Instinctively a lane was opened out to let the stretchers pass, stiffened with dried blood, and loaded with stiffer burdens. Although scarcely twelve hours had passed since the battle, most of the dead were already half naked, which would have been inexplicable, had we not seen mysterious figures prowling about under the trees on the outskirts, and others in the distance, making off with large bundles: they were the peasantry of the neighbourhood, the human vultures who had done this sacrilegious deed. The dead were collected in heaps near the places where they fell, a long trench dug beside them, and twenty or thirty laid in each. Whoever makes a pilgrimage to the battlefield of Magenta may trace, by these little tumuli, where the battle was fiercest. He will find them scattered about among the vineyards between Ponte Nuovo and Ponte Vecchio; he will see numbers about the *cascine* towards Turbigo; but most of them are in the large pits opposite the railway-station behind the yellow railing; they are the resting-places of those who fell at the entrance of the town, and on this hard-contested point itself. Little wooden crosses are erected over these tumuli, on some of which may be seen, even now, the withered flower-wreaths hung up as pious memorials by their departing comrades.

Transports of wounded are always a painful sight, but they are a thousand times more so since those instruments of torture, the iron chairs on mules, have been invented. At each step of the heavy-footed animal, every fibre of the wound is shaken. And then those lazy stumbles, obstinate backings, malicious trots—they are enough to shake the soul out of a sound body; what must they be to a man with a broken limb? And from Magenta to Novara there are thirteen or fourteen miles. It was, however, only those who were slightly wounded who were carried so far; the others were taken to Magenta, and as the next morning a railway train was sent from Milan, all the wounded were transported to that capital.

Not the least gloomy of all these gloomy sights were the long strings of prisoners who were marched off towards a large factory building, which lies near the bridge of Buffalora. It was in itself a study to look at those countenances, some elated, others downcast, some pale and exhausted, others gloomy but determined, marching erect, with that regular military step which is the boast of the Austrian army. Strings of some hundreds, accompanied by a few French infantry soldiers, and in one instance a procession of well-nigh 3,000, escorted by a small picket of cavalry. Besides these, for several days fresh prisoners were brought in, in batches of two or three, who had been wandering about in the neighbourhood, or had lost their way, or concealed themselves. They were all sent off to Novara, and from thence to Genoa and France.

As artillery had not been extensively employed, the villages and detached houses had not suffered very much. At Magenta itself, the first row towards the station showed most marks of destruction in the walls, and several were so ill-treated that they have been since pulled down and are rebuilding; for the rest, there is only here and there an occasional cannon-ball, and plenty of bullet-marks. Most ill-treated were the windows and doors, not only at Magenta, but likewise at Ponte Nuovo and Ponte Vecchio. In all the five houses which stand in the former place, by a strange caprice of the bullets, only one single pane of glass remained. The colonnade which stretches out before the house, formerly used as a passport-office by the Austrians, was a peculiar point of attraction, not only on the 5th, but likewise on the succeeding days; for before it had been collected all the knapsacks, tunics, cloaks, &c, of the fallen French soldiers which had escaped the human vultures of the neighbourhood, and were found on the field of battle. The few articles of which the French soldier's kit consists were lying there scattered about, and mixed up with all kinds of odds and ends, for which soldiers have a fancy—brushes, button-cleaners, shoe-blacking, stockings, scarfs, gaiters, pipes, tin canteens, cards, muskets, drums, caps, bearskins, *fez* caps, shirts, combs, pieces of soap, and a variety of other objects, in endless confusion. In spite of the sentries, and the continual exhortations of the officers *d'Intendance*, everyone who passed found something to suit him, and carried it off. However, far more interesting than anything else, in this odd cloth-market, were the letters and regimental books of the fallen soldiers, which were strewed about among the archives of the Austrian police-office of Magenta: those soiled pieces of paper, so full of pedantry, narrow-mindedness, and scurrility, among these others, equally soiled, but full of love, hope, and tenderness; instructions how to get hold of a wretched deserter laid upon the tender inquiries and anxieties of a mother about her son's well-being; the outpourings of a loving sister to her brother lying side by side with the copy of an order of arrest;—it was the most striking contrast of all that is best and worst in our human nature, and not exactly calculated to make one merry and cheerful.

But still that scorching June sun illuminated with his golden rays not only sad sights of misery death, and destruction, on the field of Magenta, but likewise scenes of joy, pride, and satisfaction, which animate a victorious army after the day of battle.

There, on the ridge near the railway bridge over the canal, were encamped the 3rd grenadiers, the heroes of the day, on the very spot which they had so brilliantly won and so gallantly defended. Side by side with them were their companions of glory, the brigade Picard, become brothers in the common danger. It is the sunny side of war, that among some of the worst it likewise develops some of the best feelings: devotion, friendship, trust, of slow growth and short duration in ordinary times, spring up in the midst of danger, to last as long as a breath is left. Further down, towards the bridge of Buffalora, the 1st corps march along the road—1st Zouaves *en tête*, who could take no part in the action of yesterday,—all full of ardour and emulation at the deeds of their comrades—burning with the desire to rival them. The three guns taken by the 2nd corps pass them, and with a loud cheer the long column divides to both sides of the road, and lets the trophy pass by to San Martino. The eye of the soldier becomes brighter when it has gone, and his step more elastic. Verily all was not dark on that field of Magenta on that 5th of June.

But brighter than to any one else must the day be to the emperor, who is standing at the window of the inn of San Martino, and looks down on the movement and stir below. He has taken up his headquarters there, and under the shade of the trees before the house are many of the generals who participated in the victory of the previous day. Sardinian headquarters have likewise come this way. All are reposing on laurels. The news has arrived that the enemy has evacuated Milan, and that he is in full retreat on the road to Abbiate Grasso, from which he came the previous day. He made a demonstration in the morning, and a few shots were discharged between his rear-guard and the 3rd corps facing towards Robecco. It must be sweet, this reposing on laurels; but the question is naturally suggested whether all is already done, and the time for reposing arrived, remembering that the greatest general of his own, and perhaps of any time, said that, "*Not he is the great general who wins battles, but he who knows how to take advantage of his victory.*"

No doubt the result already obtained was great. Not only was Milan freed from Austrians, but there was every reason to believe that they would evacuate the whole of Lombardy to the Mincio, without striking another blow. But were there not chances of something more? There was the defeated Austrian army retiring between a network of canals, the Naviglio Grande, the Naviglio di

ENTRY OF THEIR MAJESTIES INTO MILAN

Bereguardo, and the Naviglio di Pavia, not to count the line of the Ticino. This army was encumbered with thousands of wounded, and behind it was the heavy baggage, part of which had probably not yet passed the Ticino, or, if it had, was on the road to Pavia, which was likewise the point of retreat. What finer opportunity could there be to pursue the defeated army vigorously and immediately? There was every probability of an utter rout. Want of troops and fatigued soldiers could not be pleaded as an excuse, for there was one entire corps of three divisions, one division in another, and two others in a third, besides the Sardinian army, which had taken no part in the action. It was not indeed certain whether the Austrian army was already sufficiently demoralized to make success sure; but this was a reason for trying to ascertain this fact. It was incomprehensible that a general who conceived and executed an idea so bold as the flank movement to the Ticino should not see all this, but should act with a caution and slowness alike suited to some superannuated general of the old pedantic school. Since the battle of Solferino and the peace of Villafranca, one cannot but suspect that it was the intention of the emperor to free Lombardy, but not to crush the Austrian army. It was the politician who hampered the general.

The 5th and 6th of June were employed in massing the whole of the allied armies on the left bank of the Ticino, and in making an attempt to intercept the division of General Urban, which had been operating against Garibaldi in the lake district. To effect this, the Sardinian army was moved forward on the left wing in the direction of Monza and the Lake of Como. The 2nd corps of Marshal MacMahon advanced on the high road towards Milan, followed by the whole infantry of the Garde Inrpériale which was also again united and took up its position as reserve. The other three French *corps d'armée*, the 3rd, 4th, and 1st, were massed on the right between Robecco and the high road to Milan, beyond Magenta, so as to watch the movements of the retreating enemy and protect the passage of the Ticino, which was now effected entirely over the bridge of Buffalora and the pontoon-bridge constructed a little higher up the river. The line of battle thus formed must be kept in mind, for its principal features remain unchanged during the rest of the campaign.

There are two great arteries of communication which intersect Lombardy from west to east, from the Ticino to the Mincio; thus forming two chief lines of operation in that country. One is the highroad from Ponte di Buffalora to Milan, and from thence to Treviglio, Calcio, Brescia, and the Mincio; the other more to the south, from Pavia, by Belgiojoso, Pizzighettone, Cremona, and Bozzolo, to Mantua. By the flanking movement of the allies and the Battle of Magenta, the Austrians were cut off from the first of these two lines, and pressed towards this latter, which they have always considered as their chief line of operations. Running as it does in the vicinity of the Po, it has been provided with a series of strongholds, all of them erected at the passages over the confluents of the Po, which come down from the north almost at right angles to the latter.

The object being to out-manoeuvre rather than to beat the Austrians, who were retreating on the southern line of operation towards the Mincio, the northern was chosen by the allies for theirs. Again, keeping the object to be obtained in view, nothing could be more appropriate than this choice and the plan based on it. The northern line of operations runs in a straight line, almost to the Mincio, is consequently shorter than the southern, to which, besides, the Austrians had, under the most favourable circumstances, two marches from Abbiate Grasso. Thus there was every probability of reaching the Mincio line as soon as, if not sooner than, the enemy. In order to accomplish this, an oblique line of march was adopted, throwing forward the left wing by the road at the foot of the Alps. This movement was intrusted to the Sardinian army, who henceforth formed the left wing of the allied army. Garibaldi, who had passed into Lombardy long before the allies, was to co-operate in this movement, manoeuvring on the extreme left a little in advance of the Sardinian army. The centre, composed of the 1st and 2nd French *corps d'armée*, and the guards, infantry, as well as cavalry, and the reserve artillery, was to proceed on the main road, a little in rear of the line of march of the left wing. The right wing formed by the 3rd and 4th corps, moved *en échelon* to the centre, in order to protect this advance parallel to the line of retreat of the enemy, and to be ready to receive him should he feel inclined to molest it.

All the preparatory movements for this plan being completed, the 2nd corps, which on the evening of the 6th was already in the neighbourhood of Milan, received orders to enter that capital; and accordingly, on the morning of the 7th, Milan, maddened with joy, received its deliverers, the inevitable Turcos at their head.

The emperor, who had summoned his household on the 5th, left San Martino the next day to transfer his headquarters to Magenta. The infantry of the guard had been sent forward on the highroad to Milan, to be in readiness to accompany the emperor at his entry. Only a few companies of the *voltigeurs* remained behind to complete the task of clearing the battlefield of Magenta; for, even on the 7th, there were wounded and prisoners brought in from all sides. An officer of the staff superintended their removal to Milan by the railway, the trains on which had been running regularly to and from Magenta since the morning of the 6th. The different railway-stations at Milan not being then in connection, the Austrians could not carry away their material; and there being no railway-bridge to blow up, the line from Milan had remained almost uninjured.

And to Milan was now hastening everyone who was not tied down by duty to some other place. The transition from Magenta, the field of death, to Milan, the town of joy, in fifty-five minutes by rail, has been described in a letter which appeared in the *Times* of the 14th of June, and which, being dictated under the impression of the moment, will convey a better idea to the reader than anything which could be written now that time has somewhat effaced this first impression.

Milan, June 8

If someone had told me that just on the ninth day after my arrival at the camp at Vercelli, I should go by rail from Magenta to Milan, I should have thought him mad; and yet so it is. I arrived here yesterday afternoon with a train of wounded and prisoners. As I told you in my last, the Milanese, immediately after the Austrian evacuation, sent up a train to fetch the wounded. As they were found, they were brought in succession to the station by the soldiers, a detachment of two companies of the 1st Fusiliers of the guard. At the station the surgeons were in attendance to apply the first dressing, and the trains from Milan went to and fro to carry them off. The trains consisted of nothing but third-class carriages and goods waggons, partly covered, partly open. Those who were only slightly wounded and could walk were put into the carriages, while the others were laid in the goods waggons, which had been made as soft as the circumstances admitted by putting straw and hay at the bottom. To these the unfortunate wretches were carried, in agonies of pain caused by the motion. A large barrel of cooling drink, made of water and syrup, was near, as well as another filled with wine, with which to assuage the fiery thirst caused by their wounds. Boughs were cut to make an awning over the open goods trucks, so as to protect their miserable inmates from the rays of a real Italian sun.

This station and the railway train itself were certainly the most shocking scenes of misery which one can possibly conceive. It was the darker side of a brilliant victory—looking behind the scenes by daylight; wounded in all stages of agony and pain, only half clad, torn, dusty, and muddy in their own blood; the priests walking about with the *viaticum* to administer the last sacrament to the dying; the glazed eye of death in some showing that they had ceased to suffer, the working eyes of others and the kneeling priest before them showing that they were on the point of sighing their last; near them were others, whom you would have thought dead, had it not been for the imperceptible movement of the eye or a convulsive twist of the limb. You became involuntarily silent when you entered, and took off your cap at the sight of so much misery. Even the lively French soldiers, who ministered to the wants of these defaced specimens of humanity, became grave, and this dead silence was only broken from time to time by the solemn words of the priest, a faint sob, a frantic shriek of pain, or a weak sigh. You almost forgot that there was a victory to redeem this dark scene. And these men, who would otherwise have peacefully followed their domestic occupations, were summoned to expose themselves to all this for a cause which is not their own, which they know nothing about, nor care for. It was, indeed, a hard lot.

But it was, above all, when the wounded had to be moved to the carriages that the neighbourhood became almost intolerable. Such shrieks, such pale faces, contracted by pain, such torn limbs! The soldiers ordered to transport them seemed to forget everything in their anxiety to alleviate the pain of the sufferers. The philanthropist would have been touched by so much care, and the cynic might have sneered at the idea that the very men who had made the wounds should now try to cure the mischief. Before starting, a new distribution of drink took place, for which there was a craving. At last the train was off, and the noise of the train drowned all others, while a few turns of the wheels took us out of sight of the station. On our arrival at Milan a number of volunteer nurses were already waiting, with glasses of lemonade to assuage the burning thirst after a passage of more than an hour.

You jumped out of the carriage, and a few steps brought you into another world, from the sight of misery to that of happiness, from pale faces to radiant ones, from shrieks of misery to cries of joy mid exultation, from a few wretched suffering men to a people mad with joy, from a railway train full of mangled specimens of humanity to a large town in its best holiday attire—the windows decorated with carpets and tricolours, French and Italian; the balconies filled with the fair, greeting every new uniform as it passed, and throwing flowers upon all soldiers without distinction; the streets crowded with people hurrahing and clapping their hands at every soldier or officer, all decorated with the Italian tricolour and the French blue in the background. Among the mass you could see the French troopers, every one accompanied by several townspeople, and carried about in triumph,—carriages full of the new guests and their entertainers; civilians with the tricolour in the buttonhole, a musket on the shoulder, and a paper stuck in the hat, on which was printed 'Ordine e Sicurezza.' These were the now municipal or national guard of volunteers, who were armed with the muskets found in the citadel, and kept by the police since.

In one word, Milan was rejoicing at the retreat of the Austrians and the entry of the French, which had taken place that morning. The corps of the Duc de Magenta, the victors of the Battle of Magenta, had entered Milan.

Unlike the Revolution of 1848, when the fight lasted five days, this time the Austrians evacuated the place in the silence of night. With the experience of 1848 before them, and the allies behind them, the Austrians well knew that Milan was untenable; and several days ago, I heard one of the officers who had been taken in the Battle of Magenta say, that a revolution at Milan was expected even before they had left. The victory of the allies made this superfluous, and the Austrians took the wise step of abandoning the disaffected town. Even before the news of the defeat of the Austrians penetrated, through other sources, the aspect of the Austrians coming back from the front showed something was wrong. They had considerably changed their attitude of masters, and from the great movement among them, it could be seen that they were preparing for their retreat. They, indeed, still promenaded the seven Zouaves whom they had taken during the fight; but they came in at one gate, and, passing through the citadel, went out at the other. The *Podestà*, of the town went with them; he was too unpopular a person to remain. In the morning, when it became clear that the Austrians had left, the municipal council assumed the direction of affairs, and took measures to prevent disorder, which otherwise might have arisen. Three thousand muskets were distributed among the more respectable part of the youth, who guarded all the public buildings, and patrolled the town, to prevent disorder. These measures were sufficient to maintain tranquillity and good humour; not the slightest excess has occurred. In the beginning, the mob, thinking of 1848, began to tear up the pavement in places, to make barricades. This was immediately stopped, and nothing can be more orderly than the behaviour of the people. It is a counterpart of what happened in Tuscany, and proves that the people, if let alone, are quite capable of taking care of themselves.

With the institution of the provisional government, if we can call it so, all the trammels of the police, censorship, &c, the well-known engines of repression, have ceased to exist—

146

THE TE DEUM IN THE CATHEDRAL OF MILAN

free movement in body and mind, and yet no haranguing, speechifying, forming of clubs or anything of that kind. The council has posted up a proclamation to reorganize the old national guard; another proclamation requests the citizens to receive the army well; and a third announces the arrival of the two allied sovereigns, and it is the joy at the long-sighed-for delivery, and the reception of their deliverers, which throws everything else into the background. A town intoxicated with joy—this is the aspect of Milan at present. Ever since the entrance of the French yesterday morning the frenzy has continued. I was not here when this happened, but from all one sees now it is easy to imagine what the first sight of the French troops must have caused,—those showers of flowers, that clapping of hands, those shouts and hurrahs, in which the Milanese seem far better up than any Italians I have ever heard! The carnival lasted till late in the night, and an illumination was improvised by placing on the balconies all the lights which were inside the apartments.

The effect was striking, for it was the illumination of the whole town at the same moment—so spontaneous and sudden that it showed better than anything else how united the Milanese are in feeling, at any rate at this moment.

But it was this morning that the excitement and frenzy attained their culminating point. At eight o'clock the emperor and the king made their entry into the town. It would have been a pardonable vanity if the two sovereigns had made their triumphal entry into the Italian capital of the enemy with all the pomp which such an entry admits. Well, not only was no advantage taken of such an opportunity, but every showing-off was studiously avoided. Nobody knew, up to the last moment, when the entry was to take place, and an early hour was chosen, in order not to leave the people time to prepare for the reception. No troops preceded, giving notice beforehand that the moment was approaching. No splendid uniforms or gaudy carriages. It was simply the entry of two commanders at the head of a body of their troops. They came from the last station, Bobbiette, which is about three leagues distant, dusty and hot; a small body of cavalry and guides preceded and closed up the rear; in the midst the two sovereigns, the King of Sardinia in the middle of the road, and the emperor to his right, both followed by their staff. The shortest road was chosen to pass through the town to the Villa Bonaparte, which is near the Giardini Publici; but it was all in vain. The news of their arrival spread with the quickness of lightning, and was made patent by one frantic shout of joy, with which I might almost say the whole town gave vent to its feelings; the thousands who were already thronging the streets began with one impulse to hurry in the direction from which the shout first arose. The scene itself, while the two sovereigns actually passed, it is impossible to describe. Imagine the madness of enthusiasm, the whole heart of a people poured out before those who had delivered it from long thraldom. Such may have been the reception of those demigods of old, after killing some wild monster which had desolated the world. Not an eye remained tearless, and proud must have been the moment for both. One such moment is almost sufficient to repay for all the cares, sacrifices, and risks, without which a great work like theirs cannot be accomplished; and necessary, too, are such moments, for they give strength for new efforts. All the outward decorations disappeared before the greeting of the people; the flowers, so long prepared for the occasion, were almost forgotten in the emotion of the moment, and fell often long before those had passed for whom they had been intended. For the first time, I saw emotion pierce through that mysterious and impenetrable countenance of the emperor—he would have been more than a man had it been otherwise.

After the sovereigns had passed, the troops came and marched through the streets to the different quarters assigned to them. Among these were the first Piedmontese who had come this time into the town. Although one might have thought that, after such a gush of enthusiasm as that which greeted the sovereigns, nature must have been exhausted, the sight of the feathers of the Bersaglieri and the modest grey dress of the Piedmontese infantry seemed to have reanimated the spark. Very likely memory flew back to the year 1848-9, when this same brave little army entered the lists for Italian freedom; and perhaps a little feeling of shame arose about the last greeting Milan gave to it when it was in adversity. At any rate, there was a marked difference in the degree of warmth with which the Piedmontese troops and the French guards were received the second day. This country of laurels seems to have been stripped of that ornament, which, twined into wreaths, showered down on the heads of the Sardinian soldiers. A great deal of this distinction must be attributed to the numbers of Lombard youths who have already entered as volunteers into the ranks of the Piedmontese army. It was her own children, as well as her neighbours and friends, whom Milan greeted in the Piedmontese, and one can scarcely grudge a little more warmth in the greeting.

After the arrival of the sovereigns, the Corso, which leads from the Villa Bonaparte to the cathedral, remained thronged with people, for it was thought that the emperor and the king would go to the cathedral to celebrate a *Te Deum*. The cathedral had been already decorated for this purpose, but it does not seem that there will be anything of the kind today, for it is three p.m. while I am writing, and there is no sign of a movement.

CHAPTER 7

The Combat at Melegnano

Events succeeded each other so rapidly in this campaign, conducted with the aid of railways and electric telegraphs, that even the dullest appreciation could not help being struck by the continual and sudden contrasts which it witnessed every instant. Scarcely more than twenty-four hours had passed since the entry of the victors of Magenta, and not more than nine since Milan poured out its feelings at the feet of its idols, the emperor and the king; and while the festively-decorated town was revelling in joy, preparing for illuminations and demonstrations, eagerly expecting the *Te Deum*, which had been deferred to the next day, the distant boom of the cannon to the south-east announced a new battle, and before another hour had passed, 2,000 more human beings were lying in the town of Melegnano dead or wounded, one half of whom had passed the very same morning through Milan, and had been crowned with flowers.

The Austrians, mainly to protect their retreat on the lower road, had thrown forward their 8th corps (Benedeck), which had taken no part in the battle of Magenta, and was now ordered to Melegnano, to take up a position there, and defend the approach to the lower Adda at Lodi, from which the allies might, by the numerous cross-roads which led down from it to the lower main road of Lombardy, have operated in the flank of the retreating Austrian army.

This movement of the Austrians, while it protected their own retreat, threatened the advance of the allied armies from Milan to the Adda, and was therefore, in this sense, an offensive as well as a defensive operation; and it was absolutely necessary to dislodge

152

the Austrians from this position, and throw them back behind the Adda, before this river could be crossed. The country between Magenta and Melegnano is intersected by two large canals—the Naviglio Grande and the Naviglio di Pavia, both of which unite on the southern outskirts of the town of Milan. There are only two roads from Abbiate Grasso to Pavia which are available for an army—one by Bereguardo, and the other by Binasco—on both of which the enemy was retiring with the *gros* of his army. The passage of the French army to the Adda lay, therefore, through Milan, especially as its object was to pass this river by Treviglio on the upper road.

As soon as the movement of the Austrians on Melegnano was known, the march of the corps was hastened. The 2nd corps (Mac-Mahon), which had entered Milan on the 7th, left it again the next morning, and was directed forward on the road to Melegnano, as far as San Donato. The 4th corps (Niel), which was following, only passed by the outskirts of Milan, and was sent forward to take up a position on the road from Milan to Pavia. The infantry of the guard which accompanied the emperor, entered Milan on the morning of the 8th, and encamped on the bastions of the town, which, planted with planes and chestnuts, have become the promenade. The 1st corps (Baraguay d'Hilliers) was on the same morning still at San Pietro l'Olmo, about seven miles in the rear of Milan; while the 3rd corps (Canrobert) was watching and slowly following the movements of the enemy on the banks of the Naviglio Grande.

On the morning of the 8th, Marshal Baraguay d'Hilliers received orders to start with his corps (the 1st) from San Pietro l'Olmo, pass through Milan, and dislodge the enemy the same day from Melegnano. The 2nd corps (MacMahon), which had already gone on to San Donato, was to co-operate with him in this attack, and for this purpose was placed under his orders as the oldest marshal. After concerting with his newly-nominated colleague, the following dispositions were taken :—The 1st corps was to form the right, and the 2nd the left column; the 1st to operate against the front of the position, the 2nd against the light flank of it. The 2nd, or left, column was to begin the movement. The 1st division of it was to attack the enemy at San Giuliano, where he showed his outposts; and having dislodged him, it was to proceed to Carpianello, to pass the river Lambro there, and go on to Mediglia. The 2nd division of the same corps was to leave the highroad at San Martino, and then follow the road which, by Trulzovi and Casanova, leads to Bettolo, to the left of Mediglia, so as to turn the position of Melegnano from the left.

The 1st corps was to proceed on the highroad as far as Betolma, whence the 1st division was to go to the right by Civesio and Viboldane to Mezzano, establish there a battery of twelve guns, and direct its fire first on Pedrano, and then on the cemetery of Melegnano, which the enemy had strongly occupied with infantry as well as artillery. The 2nd division of the same corps was to leave the highroad at San Giuliano, and turn to the left, marching on San Brera, to establish there another battery of twelve guns against the cemetery situated at the entrance of the village, and likewise enfilade the road from Melegnano to Lodi.

The 2nd division was to go on, following the main road to Melegnano, and take the town, together with the 2nd and 3rd divisions, as soon as the artillery had produced due effect.

After the occupation of the village, the 1st division, leaving Melegnano to its left, was to march to Cerro, the 2nd and 3rd to Sordio, where they were to operate in conjunction with the 2nd corps, which was directed to the place by Dresano and Casalmajocco.

Nothing could be more beautifully combined than this attack— one column threatening the rear of the position and the road to Lodi from the side where it comes out of the village of Melegnano, and the divisions of the second column converging from three sides and attacking the position from both flanks and in front. Melegnano, situated at the points of junction of the branches of the river Lambro, is rendered extremely strong by these canalized little streams. The main road runs down to it almost in a straight line, and being flanked on both sides by wide and deep canals, branches of the Naviglio, forms a defile by which the village seems almost unattackable. It was, therefore, advisable to operate from the flanks; and had all these artistic combinations been carried into effect, as they were written on paper, it might have saved the French a great many men, and have produced important results.

All depended upon that great agent in strategical combinations, *time*: the flank movements had to produce their effect before the attack in front could take place, and in this respect the movement at Melegnano was a complete failure. The distance from San Pietro

BATTLE OF MELEGNANO

l'Olmo to Melegnano, about 15 or 16 miles, had to be traversed by the 1st corps. It started at five in the morning, but found the road so encumbered by the baggage of the 2nd and 4th corps, which had preceded it, that it could advance but slowly. It passed through Milan in the forenoon, and, like all the other troops, became the object of great ovations on the part of the people, who strewed their road to the battlefield with flowers, till there was not a soldier who had not a nosegay in the nozzle of his musket, not an officer but had at least one laurel-wreath, and flowers enough to form a respectable opera-bouquet. As for the superior officers, they had each the produce of a small garden before them on the saddle. The reception was such, that it made them almost forget that as yet they had not breakfasted; for such was the hurry, that they did not even wait for their coffee. The road was as much encumbered beyond as in the rear of Milan, so that it was half-past three o'clock before the 1st corps could draw up in line, and send off the two divisions to the flanks. While this movement was being executed, the 2nd division (Bazaine), which was to attack in front, halted and cooked its coffee. MacMahon's corps, on the contrary, had already begun its flank movement to the rear of Melegnano, and having found no enemy at San Giuliano, waded through the Lambro at Carpianello, and continued its way to Mediglia.

There were still more than four hours of daylight, and thus plenty of time to wait for the arrival of the flanking columns. But this was not done. Both the right and the left turning columns had found obstacles in their way. The first found not only the bridges over the canals damaged, but likewise the enemy posted at Pedriano, behind a high stone wall surrounding a large farm-house. As for the left column, it found the bridges over the Lambro broken, and the water, owing to the rain, so high, that it had to seek some time for a ford. In the meantime, the 2nd division, having taken its coffee, hastily advanced towards Melegnano, in front of which it found itself, a little after five p.m., at a distance of 1,000 yards. The Austrians had cut the road and thrown up a barricade upon it, at about 500 yards from the town, and had erected a battery at the entrance of the village itself. Just at the moment the column approached, a thunderstorm, which had been collecting, burst, and retarded the attack for about half an hour.

The Austrian guns opened out, but so little was an attack expected from the front, that the first shot was directed on the flanking columns, which were just then approaching the town, and trying to take up the position assigned to them. The 2nd division formed a line of battle; one battalion of the 1st Zouaves was sent forward, and to the plains, in skirmishing order, the 2nd battalion was ordered to put down its knapsacks and charge the enemy's battery in front of the village. The 3rd battalion, and the 33rd of the line, were to support the charge.

The Zouaves, full of desire to emulate their comrades who had taken so brilliant a part at Palestro and Magenta, and who had been long complaining of their inactivity, rushed on with even more than their usual *élan*. The enemy had occupied the approaches to the village, as well as the houses, leaving the road guarded by the skirmishers, who now received the Zouaves with a brisk fire; but they could not stop them, for on they went in one rush to the cemetery, at the entrance to the village. This is a large plot of ground, surrounded by a wall from 15 to 18 feet high, and covered outside with tombstones of black marble embedded in it. The only entrance to it is through a large massive iron gate. This cemetery the enemy occupied in force, as well as the ground planted with vines which slopes down behind it towards the Lambro. Benches surround a little chapel, which is enclosed by the wall, and ladders were placed against the enclosure, to serve as a banquette for the defenders. Yet in spite of these precautions, the resistance was not great, for the rest of the column had already penetrated into the town, and taken a large farmhouse, which forms its left entrance. From this moment till the complete evacuation of the town an hour afterwards, the combat was nothing more nor less than a street fight, entirely borne by the Zouaves and the 33rd. Every house was strongly occupied and obstinately defended. Concealed behind the windows, the enemy, sufficiently protected, directed a murderous fire on the assailants below. But on the Zouaves went, from house to house, with greater and greater fury. Their officers do not wear the Zouave costume, and had become targets for the enemy, who picked them off one after another; this maddened the soldiers to an incredible degree.

Just on the opposite outskirts of the town is a large building,

DEFENCE OF VARESE BY GARIBALDI

once a *chateau*, and lately used by the Austrians as a house of correction; it occupies one side of an open square and is surrounded by a large dry ditch. There is a double gateway to it from the square; the outer, a square tower, having evidently once been connected by a drawbridge with the inner one; a causeway now leads over it, and through this the Austrians had to make their way. They were caught by the Zouaves and a number bayoneted. Those who could get through in time ran to the garden, which leads from the courtyard into the fields. A massive iron gate separates the two, which the Austrians found means to shut. The building on all other sides is surrounded by a ditch, flanked with masonry about 15 feet high; so the Austrians could escape to the fields. The Zouaves sent bullets after them, and in their eagerness shot down in the dusk fifteen or twenty men of the 34th of the line, which formed part of the 2nd division, and was just appearing on the left flank, when the fight was almost over. The same was the case with the 1st division to the right, which, however, was able to despatch a few cannon-shot after the enemy on the road to Lodi.

By nine o'clock, the last shot had been fired, and everything was over. The Austrians were retreating on the road to Lodi, leaving one cannon and 8,000 or 9,000 prisoners in the hands of the French, and about 1,500 dead and wounded lying on the ground.

Nor was the victory cheaply bought by the French, who lost about 1,000 in killed and wounded; among them thirteen officers killed, and fifty-six wounded. The Zouaves alone had nearly 600 men. *hors de combat*, among them thirty-three officers—Colonel Toulce d'Ivoy dead, and two of the commandants mortally wounded. They had remained on horseback during the street fight, and had even kept on their white *burnuses*.

The story goes that Marshal Baraguay d'Hilliers and his staff sat down to the dinner prepared for General Benedeck and staff, who had made themselves comfortable for the evening, relying as they did on the strength of their position.

As the combat had been prolonged till dark, the wounded had to be sought for during the night, and ghastly indeed was this search by torchlight, which threw its fantastic red glare on the scene of death all around. The population, which had been concealed in the cellars during the fight, crawled out again, and were standing at the door of their houses, illuminated by the light falling upon them from inside. The rain had ceased, but on the sky thick dark clouds were still chasing each other—the air still full of that peculiar indescribable atmosphere, a mixture of gunpowder, dust, blood, and sweat, which unmistakably indicates a battlefield, and which was rendered more and more striking by its contrast with the scent arising from the vegetation saturated with rain. In this obscurity, rendered more intense by the fantastic light in one or two spots, the search was going on—or rather stumbling along over the bodies lying on the ground, guided by the groans of those who had still the strength to make themselves heard, and accompanied by the exclamations and jocular remarks of the seekers, produced by the many incidents to which the search gave rise. There was only one moment of real mirth; it was when between a heap of dead and dying an Austrian was discovered, who, with that good-natured solicitude which characterizes the French soldier on such occasions, was questioned and examined all over to detect his injury, and who turned out to be safe and sound, a discovery which caused great fun to the searchers, but not to him who was thus found out.

By daylight next day, most of the wounded were already removed, and on their way to Milan, when the burial began; most of the officers had brought with them the flowers which were strewn on their graves. The Zouaves had contrived to find deals to make coffins for their officers, and in the old Castello, which was occupied by the regiment, their corpses were laid out covered with flowers and laurel-wreaths. It made even the Zouaves thoughtful.

The sound of the cannon at Melegnano did not much disturb the Milanese on the 8th, they were too intoxicated with joy. But if the Milanese forgot in their joy that others were fighting for their cause a few miles off, they remembered that it was their duty to do everything to alleviate the sufferings of the wounded. Already, during the night, but more especially the next morning, hundreds of private carriages, from the most stylish equipage to the two-wheeled cart of the country, were sent to the battle-field as improvised ambulances; and they came back with wounded, who were taken to the private houses. Every family gave what it could afford in linen, bedding, and *charpie*; the ladies went as volunteer nurses to the hospitals, sent all kinds of dainties, and did, in fact, everything that could be desired; and all this was performed spontaneously, and with a, goodwill and readiness which showed that they knew how to appreciate the services of their "liberators."

If the Milanese had their pleasure rather spoiled by the storm on the morning of the 8th, they were indemnified by the splendid sight which the procession to the Duomo and the *Te Deum* afforded them the next day. In expectation of coming events, the street was alive from six in the morning,—an altogether unearthly hour for Milan. Soon after, the balconies began to fill with the fair and their projectiles, rose-leaves in jars, besides bouquets and wreaths. The infantry of the guard was the first to come in for its share. They came from their camping-ground near the Piazza d'Armi, traversed the streets, music in front, and then formed a line along the Corso through which the emperor was to pass to the Duomo. It rained flowers; the air resounded with enthusiastic hurrahs; everyone was radiant, the streets bright and sunny; in fact, everything beautiful and satisfactory.

At eleven a.m. all the bells in Milan begin to ring, the troops shoulder and present arms, the drums beat, the bands strike up; and through all this the sound of cheering coming nearer and nearer announces the approach of the emperor, who passes on horseback, in company with the king, through the Corso. At the entrance of the Duomo the clergy are waiting to receive the two sovereigns, and the whole ceremony passes off as these things usually do. Only the attitude of the people was interesting, for rarely was there a thanksgiving in which so many hearts sincerely joined; not only those privileged to go inside, but the thousands and thousands outside. And then the splendid Duomo showing off its delicate marble face against the pure-blue sky; the magnificent troops, still surrounded with all the halo of a recent victory; and an Italian sun, hot indeed, but brilliant. It was a sight such as it rarely falls to the lot of man to see.

During the rest of the day thousands and thousands flocked to the Porta Lodana, where the wounded were coming in from the field of Melegnano; and in the evening everyone was in the Corso to see or take part in the ovation prepared for King Victor Emmanuel. A procession of thousands and thousands assembled on the Place before the Theatre of La Scala with music; tricolours, inscribed *"Viva l'Unione!" "Viva il nostro Ré!"* and no end of torches, and proceeded through the illuminated and festively-decorated streets to the Corso, where the king had taken up his residence in the Palazzo Busca. With every step this gigantic crowd swelled more and more, until the whole Corso was one dense mass of human beings in slow progress. This crowd, already sufficiently animated, became more and more so by the hurrahs with which it was received, as it passed under the windows and balconies filled with people, shouting and waving handkerchiefs and tricolour flags. The crowd moved on without an accident or even a word of quarrel, though not a soldier or policeman was to be seen; women and children, as well as men, cheered the king to their hearts' content, as he appeared on the balcony, and then went away again singing and hurrahing. And this was the people of Milan, who could only be kept in order six days before by gendarmes, bayonets, prisons, and spies!

The next day, the 10th, the emperor went to the battlefield of Melegnano, but was back again in the course of the day, and in the evening both he and the King, attended a concert which was given at the Theatre la Scala. Although the time of illuminations was gradually passing away, the Corso and all the streets were illuminated. In spite of the drizzling rain, large crowds were assembled before the theatre. Towards eight o'clock, their Majesties, accompanied only by their usual escort, drew up in an open carriage, amid the hurrahs of the assembled multitude. The enthusiasm, which might reasonably have exhausted itself, seemed greater than ever. The interior of the beautiful building itself was of course illuminated a *giorno*, and the boxes filled with the best society of Milan, resplendent in their toilets and intermixed with the greatest variety of uniforms. The *coup d'oeil* was indeed magnificent, when at the entry of the two sovereigns all this brilliant mass stood up with one shout of enthusiasm, waving handkerchiefs and bouquets, and laughing, crying, cheering, as any mob would in the streets. On witnessing this indescribable scene of gratitude, joy, happiness, homage,—one might almost say worship,—it could not be forgotten that within fifty yards of the scene of this wild enthusiasm is the Casa Creppi, on the balcony of which stood Charles Albert

ATTACK OF S. FERMO BY GARIBALDI

and Victor Emmanuel, when, after the disasters of August, 1818, they were fired upon from the crowd below. Such are the strange changes in human affairs.

This representation at the Scala concluded the joyous holiday which the Milanese had kept ever since the Austrians departed, and the next day, the 11th, Milan began to assume again its wonted aspect, minus the Austrian soldiers, who were only found as prisoners in the Castello, and *plus* some thousands of tricolours, floating from windows and balconies, and numberless tricolour rosettes, with which every man, woman, child, and priest was decorated. The shops, which had been shut while everyone was making a holiday, began to open again, so that it was difficult to suppose that this was a town that had changed its ruler less than a week ago, and which was just busy establishing a new government. However, the great alteration that had taken place, could not be very well mistaken by any one in the habit of looking at the aspect of the population. The scowling, censorious, and petulant populace of Milan had been transformed into a joyous, impressionable, and good-natured people. The transition from one rule to another was sudden and without a struggle; none of the passions which are sure to appear in every popular movement had been roused. It was like the sudden realization of a dream long hoped for, and ardently desired; and the Milanese awoke one morning and found this cherished dream a reality.

GARIBALDI

The size of this work does not allow us to follow this gallant general in all his movements, but no account of the Italian war would be complete without some reference to the important part played by the Cacciatori delle Alpi. They were the only representatives of the popular element of Italy in this war.

In order to regulate the Italian movement, and not to let it run wild, as it did in 1848, the two sovereigns put themselves at the head of it. They kept down systematically all fermentation, prevented agitation, and the people, trusting to their powerful interference, gave scarcely any sign of life while their fate was being decided. They had not trusted in vain, for town after town, and district after district, were rid of the Austrians by the gradual advance of the allies, and without any danger or sacrifice on their part. There were, indeed, numbers of youths, who, even before the war broke out, went over to Piedmont and enlisted; but this was the act of individuals, as such, and not of the people collectively. The latter had only occasion to show their spirit by enthusiastic displays of welcome and gratitude to the allies.

It was only on the southern slopes of the Alps, that the popular element was called early into play, and Garibaldi with his Cacciatori delle Alpi was to lead this movement. Their mission was to rouse the population in the mountains, and with their assistance drive out the Austrians. This mission was in connection with the great plan of advance, for while the main column of the allies advanced in the plain, Garibaldi had to operate on their left flank, or rather, left front. With a body of from 3,000 to 4,000 volunteers, he crossed the Ticino at the foot of the Lago Maggiore, on the night of the 23rd—24th of May, that is, several days before the advance of the allies began. The people of Lombardy had long before been prepared for his arrival, thanks to the exertions of the Società Nazionale Italiana, which had its ramifications all over Italy. Arms were to have been sent through Switzerland, but they were detained at the frontier, and never arrived at their destination. But the moment chosen for crossing was very favourable, for the Austrians, who seemed as usual to have suspected nothing, had made no preparations to receive the Cacciatori delle Alpi. The latter, therefore, leaving their baggage behind, crossed in boats to the Lombard side of the Ticino, and were next morning at Varese, just midway between the Lago Maggiore and the Lago di Como. Garibaldi addresses a proclamation to the people of Lombardy, calling them to arms, the alarm-bells are sounded in all villages, and numbers of youth flock under his standard as volunteers. A national guard is formed in the town and its neighbourhood, and armed with muskets, which had been previously smuggled over.

A small Austrian detachment with two guns, the only force which was at Gallatari, advanced to Sesto Calende to cut off the retreat of the Cacciatori, but they were received by a party of the latter left in charge of that place, and had to retire. This was on the 29th.

The next day Garibaldi himself is attacked at Varese by a strong column coming from Como. The town had been barricaded, and after some hours of fruitless efforts the Austrians retire and are pursued for several miles. They retire, towards Como, one part of them occupying Camerlata, where the terminus of the Como-Milan railway is, and the others intrenching themselves on the position of S. Formo, an isolated church, and a *cascina* on the road from Lugano to Como. This position was of great importance, for the frontier of Switzerland coming down close to the western shores of the Lake Como, the position of S. Formo, which forms an isolated hill between the two, was necessary for Garibaldi, in order to secure his retreat from Como in case the Austrians brought up larger forces.

He attacked it consequently on the 27th of May, and after considerable loss in officers as well as men, got possession of it, and on the same evening entered Como. The next morning the telegraph was re-established with Turin. The whole country declared for Victor Emmanuel. The Sardinian commissioner Venosta Visconti, is recognized, and takes the organization of the country in his hands.

But the Austrians had already despatched General Urban with his flying corps to catch Garibaldi, and in consequence it became urgent to send reinforcements. A Sardinian detachment was sent to Castelletto, at the foot of the Lago Maggiore opposite Sesto Calende. Urban advanced in two columns, one against Garibaldi, and the other against Castelletto, while the steamers on the Lago Maggiore were to have prevented the crossing of the Cacciatori higher up. There it was hoped to catch the Cacciatori delle Alpi, or else to force them to retire into Switzerland, where they would be disarmed. The position was by no means brilliant; but, bold as usual, Garibaldi, although without a single gun, conceived the idea of attacking Lavino, a fort on the eastern shore of the Lago Maggiore, which was occupied by several hundred Austrians, with several guns. The night was chosen for the purpose, but the attack which took place in the night of the 30th—31st did not succeed, and he had twenty-four hours of great anxiety. Urban, with one column, was in Varese on the 31st, and the other column at Sesto Calende.

But the 1st of June the French were at Novara, and on the morning of the 2nd, the Austrian army was falling back. On the same day, Garibaldi, with the Cacciatori, was again in Varese, and in the night of the 2nd and 3rd again in Como.

On the 4th was the battle of Magenta, and from that moment we see Garibaldi, with the Cacciatori delle Alpi, always in advance of the left flank of the allies, rousing and organizing the country on the southern slopes of the Alps, recruiting and following on the heels of the Austrians. Before the allies entered Milan he was in Lecco on the eastern branch of Lake Como. Before the allies had crossed the Adda, he was at Bergamo; and while the allies were crossing the Adda, he was already in Brescia.

These are facts which speak for themselves, and bear testimony to the boldness and resources of the commander, as well as the bravery of his troops. Before the war in Italy there was an apprehension abroad that the Italians would not fight. The bravery of the Piedmontese army was not of course questioned, but since 1848 the volunteers had not a very good name, as with some brilliant exceptions, they did not show fight well. Garibaldi's troops formed an exception, and kept up their renown in the late war. To any commander, but, above all, to the leader of light troops like Garibaldi, the confidence of the soldier is one of the most necessary qualifications. General Garibaldi possesses this to an incredible degree; he seems to know how to inspire every one about him with blind obedience, unbounded trust, and almost affection.

His name, his position as the representative of the Italian popular element, attached to his standard all the more enthusiastic part of the youth. The Sardinian government, not very favourably disposed towards anything not belonging to the regular army, tried to draw away the volunteers from the Cacciatori. Those only resisted who were from the first determined; and thus it came that, unlike other irregular corps, the Cacciatori were rather a *corps d'élite*. It was only thus possible to undertake and accomplish successfully the mission of hovering on the flanks of the enemy and insurging the country.

Aided by the Sardinians and the spirit of his troops, Garibaldi was able to realize the true mission of light troops to perfection. Now on the flank, now on the rear, now on the flank of the enemy, and appearing on points where he was least expected, he owed to this mobility his escape from the superior forces which were sent against him.

CHAPTER 8

The Advance to the Mincio

After the victorious combat at Melegnano, we see the same slackness in the pursuit of the allies as after Magenta. In spite of the recollections suggested by the neighbourhood of Lodi and its bridge, there seemed to be no wish to revive them, although this might probably have been done even with greater success than in the famous campaign of 1796, which first established the military renown of General Bonaparte. The Austrians were securely crossing the Adda on the 8th, the day of Melegnano, and on the two successive days, in three great columns, into which they had divided their army. The 8th corps (Benedeck) and a part of the 7th (Zobel) forming the right wing, and as it were a vanguard, of the army, were preparing to cross at Lodi; while the centre, 1st, 2nd, 3rd, and the remaining part of the 7th, were crossing on pontoon-bridges, constructed lower down at Vinzasca and Formigava; finally, the left wing, composed of the 5th and 9th corps, and of the garrisons of Pavia and Piacenza, was making towards Pizzighettone. One glance at the map will show that the Adda, which flows as far as Lodi in a southerly direction, here takes a south-easterly course. This made it necessary for the Austrians to keep Lodi until the rest of the army had crossed lower down. The French were, on the evening of the 8th, already at Sordio, not more than seven miles from Lodi, with the 1st and 2nd *corps d'armée*. The 4th corps was within easy distance on the road to Pavia; the 2nd corps not much further back to its right, and the Imperial Guard at Milan.

It seemed an almost irresistible temptation to fall upon this army crossing the river; that is, engaged in one of the most awkward positions in which a beaten army can possibly be attacked. Ignorance of the movements of the Austrians can scarcely be alleged as a reason for neglecting this opportunity, for if the allied armies could gather no intelligence in this part of Lombardy, no army can ever get information. The Austrians themselves seemed to expect a pursuit, for at the news of the advance towards Melegnano, on the 8th, they returned to Pavia, which they had abandoned two days before, thus preparing to make head against the French army coming down from Milan. But this, instead of being a reason for stopping the pursuit, was, on the contrary, rather one to hasten it, for a successful battle would have cut off the Austrians from the Mincio, and thrown them back on the Po. Everything leads to the belief that the intention was rather to manoeuvre the Austrians out of Lombardy than to annihilate their army; and, with this view, the plan of advancing on the upper road to the Mincio had been adopted, and the whole Sardinian army sent off in that direction. The movement towards Lodi was only made with the double object of ascertaining whether the Austrians really intended to retreat; and then of dislodging them from a position flanking the Upper Adda, which the allied armies intended to pass.

The Austrians, seeing that the French made no attempt to disturb their retreat, resumed their march on the 9th; and on the evening of the next day the whole Austrian army had crossed the Adda between Lodi and Pizzighettone, that is on a line of fully fifteen miles, and considerably more if the tortuous course of the river and of the roads are taken into account. In the night of the 10th—11th the bridge of boats at Lodi was destroyed, and the Austrian army concentrated between the Serio and the Oglio.

While the Austrian main army thus effected its retreat over the Adda, General Urban, with his division, had had time to withdraw from the exposed position he had held against Garibaldi in the mountains, and to escape the Sardinian forces sent against him. He recrossed the Adda, destroying the bridges at Cassano, Vapio, and San Pietro, retiring in the direction of Bergamo and Romano.

On the 11th the Sardinian army, which had been concentrated in the direction of Vimercate, threw pontoon bridges over the Adda at Vaprio, at the confluence of the river Brembo with the Adda. The same day the French bridged over the Adda at Cassano, where the main road to Brescia, as well as the railway-line, passes this river. It is needless to say that no opposition was found at either place. The Austrians had made up their minds long ago that nothing was to be done but to retire and concentrate their forces on the Mincio; and as the allies did not choose to disturb their retreat, and left them sufficient time to carry out this intention, they had of course no reasons for making themselves particularly disagreeable. Besides this, the left bank of the Adda, like that of almost all the feeders of the Po, is considerably lower than the right; consequently, except in case of necessity, not a very advisable line of defence. Thus by this account we see the two hostile armies marching almost side by side on parallel roads, often only divided from each other by a few miles; each taking every precaution to guard against a surprise, yet neither much disposed to hurt the other.

In order to understand these apparently strange tactics of the allies, it must be remembered that the passage of the Adda by the Austrians had altogether changed the circumstances of the case: so that what then seemed commanded by every military consideration, would now have been untimely rashness. It was then the question of pursuing a beaten army retiring over a difficult country, with a river of some size to cross; to fall upon it before it had time to recover from the blow already inflicted, and from the confusion caused by the long precipitate retreat from the Lomellina, first in one, then in another direction. The allied army was then in the neighbourhood of Milan, which, with its resources, became, as it were, a secondary base of operations, and from this new centre they could easily have provided for their army as far as the Adda or the line of the Po. Finally, if the allies succeeded in defeating the Austrian army under these circumstances, there was a fair chance of its being completely dispersed before it ever reached the neighbourhood of the famous *quadrilatère*, which would then have been defended by only two corps, the 6th at Verona, and the 11th at Mantua. All these circumstances had now altered. A week had elapsed since the Battle of Magenta, during which the Austrians had had time to send away their heavy baggage and wounded, and make all the necessary preparations for their retreat; so that the allies had no longer to deal with an army in confusion. They were at liberty, if possible, to reproduce this state of things; but this was not so easy, for the Austrians had gained a full day and more in their march, and the distance to the Mincio was not sufficient to make up for this advantage. The allies could no longer force the Austrians to accept a battle. The second difficulty was the question of resources. The nearer the Austrians came to the Mincio, the nearer they were to their base of operations, while the allies were more and more separated from theirs. For an army of 30,000 to 35,000 men living on requisitions and levying contributions, like the armies of the first French Republic, this was a minor consideration; but an army at least four times the size wishing to conciliate the population of the country, had to bring up nearly everything it wanted. Now, it is proved by experience that an army like that of the allies cannot do so *for any length of time* beyond fifteen or twenty miles, without enormously encumbering itself with waggon-trains. Had the railway been available, it would have been different; but all the bridges had to be repaired; there was scarcely any *matériel* left; and to bring up the latter, the two stations at Milan had to be connected.

All these considerations might, however, have been set aside, had it only been necessary to make a forced march in order to rejoin and beat the enemy. But the time had passed for this, and the Austrian army once on or behind the Mincio, the allies had no longer to deal with an army in the open field, but with one behind fortified lines, carefully prepared, which, consequently, no one could hope to take at a rush. It was at the best a work of weeks, if not months, which required considerable preparations for feeding the army, besides all the material for a siege. Therefore, when the Austrian army had once passed the Adda, a precipitate advance would have brought the allies to the Mincio unprepared to continue their task.

Whatever may be thought of the rapidity with which the French army appeared on the scene of action in Italy, France was not prepared for war: the regiments which had to leave were, in fact, on a peace footing, except those which came from Algeria. They had scarcely two-thirds of their strength, the rest being on what is called *congé renouvelable*; that is, after serving three or four years, the men are allowed to go on furlough, which is renewed for short periods until they have served their time. Most of these men were called in after the war began, and they were just arriving when the army left the neighbourhood of Milan. It was an additional object to give them time to join their regiments.

The siege-train was behind owing to the same cause, or because no one expected it would be wanted so soon; at any rate, when the army left Milan, the greater part of it was only passing the Mont Cenis. The gun-boats for the lake had, indeed, arrived at Genoa; but they could not be brought up except by railway, and had, therefore, to wait for its completion.

In one word, a pursuit immediately after the Battle of Magenta, and before the Austrians had crossed the Adda, was terminating the campaign without the *quadrilatère*; and following the Austrians after they had crossed this river, was preparing for the attack of the *quadrilatère*.

The king left Milan on the evening of the 11th, and transferred his headquarters to Vimercate. The emperor left next morning for Gorgonzola, whither the Imperial Guard followed him. The corps which had taken part in the movement towards Lodi came up one after another, and crossed at Cassano and a little lower down. Next day the king moved his head-quarters after his army, which had crossed at Vaprio. The emperor moved his to Cassano, and on the 14th to Treviglio. The king, after a flying visit to Bergamo, established his headquarters at Palozzuolo on the Oglio on the same day, and the next day at Castegnato, before Brescia. The emperor was on the 15th at Calcio, on the Oglio, and on the 10th at Ospitaletto. Thus, it will be observed, the left wing of the army was always one day's march in advance of the centre. The right wing, formed of the 4th and 3rd French corps, similarly hung back.

In this manner the allied armies advanced from the Mincio to the river Mella, close to Brescia. It was nothing but a military promenade, a rich country, easy stages, not yet too hot, and only an occasional shower to lay the dust.

The following extract from a letter which appeared in the *Times*, dated from the banks of the Adda, will give an idea of the impression produced at the time, by this part of the warfare :—

> Thus both parties are preparing with equal vigour for the great occasion. In the meantime, until it happens, the

allied armies, at any rate, have an agreeable time of it, in this fertile and beautiful Lombard plain, through which they are marching. It is like an agreeable promenade in a park. Although the country between Milan and the Adda is similar to that further west, yet the richness of the vegetation, combined with the perfection of cultivation, gives it an entirely different character. Thus, you have the long, straight *chaussées*, it is true, but they are not those monotonous sunburnt roads, with equally monotonous rows of willows, or naked, closely-planted poplars, cropped close as charity-boys; here you have a road protected in most parts by high, full-spread chestnuts, poplars, and elms, which impart shade even at noonday. Two little ditches, with clear flowing streams on either side, lend additional freshness, and vivify a dense mass of brushwood and creepers at the foot of the high trees. Besides the wild vine, which gracefully creeps up under the branches of its more powerful neighbours, you find there all your old acquaintances—the nut, the raspberry, the cranberry, and every variety of the three, while at their feet, near the fresh water, nestle a number of wild flowers in all their varied garments. The side roads are no longer those tiresome nursery-garden rows, which must have served as models for the background in the pictures of the early Italian school. The richness of the vegetation has transformed them into delicious cool country lanes. The rice-fields have quite disappeared, and the cornfields are much less frequent. Instead of them the eye roams over large plots of grass, chiefly thick Lucerne, which is grown in large quantities in this country, renowned for its dairies. The formal enclosures beyond are so completely hidden by the richness of the brushwood and the free growth of the trees, that they seem the borders of a considerable forest, just sufficiently cleared to admit the grass plot. All this mass of verdure is animated by the song of the nightingale, the blackbird, and lark, who seem to have forgotten the numerous sportsmen of Lombardy, or, perhaps, think that while the cry is '*Morte ai Tedeschi!*' they, as good patriots, have nothing to fear. From Milan all along to the Adda the villages succeed each other almost with as much rapidity as in the neighbourhood of London, only they are picturesque Italian villages, and not uniform suburban hamlets. Besides these, you almost every moment meet one of the *cascine*, or large detached farmhouses, or see them in the distance, peeping out of the trees beyond the road. Every one is the centre of groups of peasants, who seem to have forgotten their work in their anxiety to have a look at the troops. Everywhere you are greeted by the sound of music and glasses, gaping crowds saluting and crying '*Evviva*,' troops reposing and refreshing themselves; the whole looks like going to a fair.

And through this jubilee the soldiers have to march by easy stages. When they halt for the day they encamp in the green fields to the right and the left, the tents are soon pitched, there is plenty of wine, bread, and meat, plenty of wood to cook with, and water everywhere. A detachment goes to the village to fetch clean straw, and the bivouac is as comfortable as can be. Now and then, indeed, a shower comes down to spoil the fun, but no one cares much about this while there is plenty to eat and drink, and the next morning the sun does the rest. Not the least important part of the afternoon's business is foraging for dainties, which is pleasant work among such numbers of rich farms; eggs, fowls, and milk are never wanting, nor is the payment at full market price only, but often rather more. If it goes on like this, the peasant will soon lose his fear of war, which, in his mind, is always equivalent to giving without receiving.

The stir, animation, and easy life which the army leads at present, are, it seems, contagious, for everywhere you see volunteers, whom you can recognize by the tricoloured feathers in the hat, and often a piece of printed paper behind it, with '*Cacciatori delle Alpi*,' printed on it. The name of Garibaldi, the less severe discipline, as it is supposed, and the romantic character which attaches to his troops, all seem to be so many allurements, which take much more than the regular military service in the regiments. With all this the good people, I think, rather deceive themselves, for the Cacciatori delle Alpi have just as much regular drilling to undergo before they join as if they were regular soldiers of the line of his Majesty Vittorio Emmanuele II. Those who are under the superintendence of the captain of the depot at Como have, I dare day, found this out by this time.

The French soldier has invented, or rather had invented for him, the word *grognard* (grumbler), and of course specimens of it were not wanting even during this advance; but as far as one could judge, there was not much ground for it. Although the stages were easy, the rapidity of the movement was still too great to allow the drawing of regular supplies from the country, by means of contracts or ready-money purchases; and most articles had to be brought from great distances. To facilitate this, an auxiliary train was organized in the beginning of the war for each of the two armies, by means of contractors, who supplied the carts of the country. It answered well; the men being proprietors of their cattle, took good care of them, and, even after the comparatively hard work which they had, horses and mules arrived on the Mincio in a very fair condition. The men themselves gave no trouble; they were kept in order by the agents of their employers, and there was no trace of the excesses by which these bodies of men usually distinguish themselves.

Only, in spite of this auxiliary train, it could not be helped if biscuit or rice had now and then to be given to the soldiers instead of bread, in the more outlying divisions of the army. And if there is a privation the French soldier feels more than any other, it is the want of bread. Meat, the soldier had every day fresh; a number of cattle had been apportioned to each division, and they followed with the baggage. The troops always had coffee, which plays a great part in the life of the French soldier, and is to him what grog is to the Englishman; and far better is it. This is an experience which the French have derived from their African campaigns, where dysentery and ague forced them to choose a substitute for wine and spirits: it was found in coffee; and so fond is the French soldier of it, that he will almost prefer being without bread to missing his coffee. As for wine, of which he ought to have had two rations a day, he had none for the last two days of the march.

It is well known that the French soldier carries his own *tente d'abri,* which is calculated to contain four men, each of whom carries a piece of it. The officers, during the first part of the march, had to leave their baggage behind them, and tents, as well. Sheds, made of branches of trees, supplied their place. At Milan, however, they got back their tents and baggage, which they thenceforth kept.

The process of preparing for the night's rest was simple enough. As soon as a column arrived at the point of its destination, there was a requisition sent in to the town or village for hay or straw, and a *bon,* payable by the *Intendance,* given for it. As it sometimes happened that the authorities were slow and the soldiers sleepy, now and then they did not resist the temptation of helping themselves to the next haystack or of carrying off some sticks from the provision of wood hoarded up in the farm-houses; but these were rare cases, except, indeed, with some whom the women of the country described as wearing petticoats, and who are even now well remembered. It used to enrage the soldier, to fight for the freedom of a country, and then to be grudged a bit of wood to cook his supper, or an armful of hay to sleep upon after his fatigue.

The peasantry of Lombardy, certainly, did not particularly distinguish itself by the welcome it gave to its deliverers; but it soon found out the source of revenue which an army in march, and forbidden to plunder, becomes for a country. And in this respect the late Italian campaign was, probably, unlike any other whichever took place; instead of the military plundering the inhabitants, according to time-honoured traditions, the latter plundered the soldiers.

It was a curious sight to see the peasantry as indifferent (except where there was something to gain) as if it had no concern at all with what was passing. The labourers in the fields on both sides scarcely looked up when the columns passed along the road, but continued their work as if they had been accustomed to see armies all their life. However, the towns made up by their enthusiasm for the passive indifference of the peasantry.

The only obstacle by which the Austrians tried to arrest the march of the victorious army of the allies was the destruction of the railway and other bridges. Thus all the bridges of the Adda were blown up; between the Adda and the Chiese, however, those over the Serio Oglio and Mella were left standing. This destruction of bridges was of considerable moment, as far as the railway bridges were concerned, for they deprived the allies for some time of those means of rapid communication. As for the other bridges, it was scarcely of any consequence, for rarely had an army a more efficient pontoon train than that of the allies. They used simple wooden punts of about twenty-five to thirty feet in length, and nine in width. Each pontoon was carried, together with the material belonging to it, on a waggon drawn by four horses, and had a slide on which it was let down: no accident ever occurred with them, and they added very little to the baggage of the army. As soon as the army had passed, and often even before, *ponts de chevalet* were made, and the pontoon bridges then removed; so that, in spite of the numerous rivers which had to be bridged over, and the rapidity of the advance, there were always sufficient pontoons in readiness to meet any emergency. The means taken to repair the railway bridges were, somehow or other, not so successful. Remembering how quickly railway accidents are repaired in England, the time from the 4th of June to the 1st of July seems rather long for repairing one bridge at Vercelli, another at Valenza, a third at Buffalora, a fourth at Cassano, and a fifth over the Chiese at San Marco. All these bridges had one or two arches blown up, but in all of them the piers supporting the arches had remained above water, thus making the repairs trifling.

When the allies in pursuit of the Austrian army arrived on the banks of the Mella, a halt was made to concentrate the forces. They were approaching the Mincio country, and before them lay the plain of Montechiaro, which begins a few miles beyond Brescia,; the allies had arrived at the first point at which the Austrians could make a stand. It is necessary to know the importance of the plain of Montechiaro as a position, as well as the character of the Mincio country, in order to understand further operations.

It is the river system of Upper Italy, regulated by canalization, which imparts fertility, and determines the character of the plains of Lombardy. With long dry summers, and only periodical heavy rains in autumn and spring, the plains of Lombardy would be a parched desert during a great part of the year, were it not for the system of artificial irrigation, which dates from time immemorial, together with the laws of water-right, so important in that country. This system of irrigation renders the greater part of the Lombard plain particularly unfavourable to the movement of large bodies

ENTRY OF THE KING OF SARDINIA INTO BRESCIA

of troops. The ground is so cut up by the canals, and so shut in by trees, that it seems almost a hopeless task to execute evolutions on a large scale, or to direct field operations on it. But there are a few spots even in the plain where the ground is either too high, or the river too far off, or too scanty, to furnish the means for this artificial fertility. The first of these plots on the line of retreat of the Austrians, was the plain of Montechiaro, situated between the river Mella and the Chiese. The range of mountains which separates the valleys of these two rivers, ceases abruptly about Brescia, leaving only a few detached longitudinal ridges scattered about the plain. The most important of these is that on which lies the village of Castenedolo; this ridge intersects the upper part of the plain just about the middle. In the western half of this latter, which begins at Brescia, or rather a little before it, there are the usual Lombard fields, with their ditches and rows of trees, more or less dense, out of which here and there peeps a *cascina* or a mill. The view is everywhere shut in, so that there are only rare opportunities of feasting the eye on the mountains which rise in bold grand outlines on the left. The road from Brescia to Montechiaro, and thence to the Mincio, leads through Castenedolo. On approaching this latter place, there is a steep ascent in the road, leading up to the ridge, on which the village lies. After traversing the village, the road descends with equal abruptness, and the plain of Montechiaro opens out. The trees, those constant companions in the Lombard plains, disappear all of a sudden about half a mile beyond the village; and then succeeds an open plain, on which for several miles there is no trace of them,—grass-plots, cornfields, and even pasture-ground, monopolizing the whole space, except only faint traces of half-effaced dry ditches and several dirty white lines of road. This open Campo, as it is called, is several miles in width and length, and is bordered on the opposite side by the banks of the Chiese, which are marked by the reappearance of trees, behind which rises a line of low but abrupt hills, skirting the opposite or left bank of the Chiese, and beginning at Castenedolo to the right, until they lose themselves in the mountains on the left, which are now seen in all their picturesque grandeur, true children of the glaciers; these hills are all detached in groups. The two most prominent among them are that of Montechiaro, and of Calcinato, standing out distinctly on the horizon, with their churches and detached houses on the summit forming a landmark afar. They can be seen from the hills above Brescia, and likewise from the hill near Volta on the Mincio.

Certainly, for an enemy strong in cavalry, and determined to have a decisive battle, no fairer ground for meeting could be found, except, perhaps, that immediately behind it in the hills of the Mincio country and the plain of Medole.

The southern shores of the lake of Garda are skirted by successive ranges of hills, more or less following the outlines of the lake, and each successive range increasing in height, until on the last outskirts towards the plain they rise to a height of at least 5,000 to 6,000 feet above the latter. All this hilly country, through which the Mincio breaks on its way to the south, has evidently been formed by the deposits of the lake, when perhaps the whole plain of Upper Italy formed part of it. The hills are an agglomeration of gravel and boulders of granite and trap-rock, generally of the size of a 12-pound shot, but in some few cases much larger. Even before approaching the hills, one may guess of what they consist, for all the buildings in their neighbourhood are constructed of smooth round stones polished by water.

The outer edge of these hills begins at Lonato, about four or five miles behind the Chiese, and runs down in a southerly direction to Castiglione. At this latter place, still following the general outline of the southern shores of the lake, it makes a sudden bend to the south-east as far as Volta, in the neighbourhood of which the Mincio leaves the hills and comes out into the plain of Mantua. On the other side of the Mincio the hills begin at Valeggio, and again following the outline of the lake, pass by Custoza, Somma Campagna, and Sona, to Bussolengo, on the Adige. Every one of these names recalls to the memory one or more battles, while between these outer points of the range and the lake itself there is scarcely a village which has not been the scene of one or more engagements during the wars of modern times. The reason is that the range along the southern shores of the lake of Garda defends the approaches and passages of the Upper Mincio, and forms, as it were, an advanced work to the position of the Mincio and the *débouché* of the valley of the Adige from the Tyrol.

It is the hilly nature of the Upper Mincio, and its vicinity to the defile of the Adige, which make the Mincio line of such vital importance to a power possessing the Tyrol; for it is a kind of *place d'armes*, fortified by nature, from which it can command the plain of Upper Italy down to the Po.

When Austria first gained possession of Lombardy, in the last century, if she did not quite overlook the importance of the Mincio country, she certainly does not seem to have understood its real value as an almost impregnable debouche from the Tyrol; for instead of concentrating her efforts on the defile of the Adige, the plateau of Verona, and the hills of the Upper Mincio, she wasted all her strength on Mantua on the lower Mincio, which never prevented her from being driven out of Lombardy. From 1796 till 1815 there was time enough to see and learn, and when Austria returned to Italy she seems to have understood the value of this position, for greater attention was paid to the really important points. But it is above all since the war with Piedmont in 1848-9, that everything was done to secure the possession of this debouche. Verona, which had before been in a secondary position, now received an importance which it never before possessed. The plateau of Rivoli was strongly fortified, and Peschiera, situated on the point where the Mincio nears the lake, considerably enlarged.

It is as an outwork to these positions that the ranges of hills along the southern shores of the Lago di Garda play a considerable part.

There are three main roads across the Mincio: one in the south, which, coming from Pavia, skirts the Po, and passes right through the fortress of Mantua; and two to the north. Both of these latter start from Brescia. The more northerly of the two goes in a straight line on Lonato, winds along the hills which begin at that place, to the shores of the lakes, passes through Peschiera, over the Mincio, and thence leads to Verona.

The other road passes through the plain of Montechiaro, crosses the Chiese at the village of the same name, and passes through Castiglione, just on the south-western outskirts of the Mincio hills. Leaving Castiglione, it takes a south-easterly direction across the open Campo di Medole to Goito, where it passes the Mincio. Besides these two main passages there are several by-roads over the Mincio, coming all either from Lonato or Castiglione, and passing the river at Salionze, Monzambano, and Valleggio.

The direction of these roads forms an important part of the system of defence of the Mincio, and they had been prepared and maintained by the Austrians with a view of restricting as much as possible the approach of an attacking army to a few points. The nature of the country considerably aided the carrying out of this design. To begin with, more than half the Mincio—namely, all the lower part of it, from Goito to Governolo, close to the Po—is so surrounded by marshes, that it is quite impassable for an army, and in the centre of this part lies the fortress of Mantua, forming the only point of passage.

In the north, all the main roads coming from the west and south-west have been centred in Brescia, and then led to the range of hills skirting the lake. An army, therefore, wishing to pass the Mincio must either attack Mantua or else pass through or close to this range of hills. These hills are just sufficiently elevated to give an *appui* to the defender, and yet not so steep as to hinder him in his movements; they are, in fact, a succession of most formidable lines of defence. While these hills are held, especially the extreme westerly points of them at Lonato and Castiglione, no army coming from the west can pass to the Mincio without compromising its line of retreat in the most awkward manner. But even if those two advanced points should be lost, a determined adversary can, in this hilly country, almost at every step, find new positions in the front and flank of the advancing army. Indeed, he must find them, if he wishes to defend the passage of the Mincio at all; for the line of river from Peschiera to Goito is too long, and the volume of water too insignificant to form a serious obstacle to a large advancing army.

The Austrians had well understood the value of these hills, for they had long chosen this as the favourite manoeuvring-place for their army in Italy during the concentration they were in the habit of having every autumn.

Taking all this into consideration, it was natural to expect the Austrians in position somewhere in or about the Mincio hills, unless it was proved that they were already too demoralized to stand in the open field, which there was no ground to suppose. For this reason the army, which had hitherto advanced in marching order, was now placed in fighting order.

On the 14th of June the Austrians retreated across the Chiese, leaving behind only General Urban, who had protected their extreme right. The 5th and 9th corps, which had formed their left wing, alone withdrew on the lower main road towards Mantua; the remaining five *corps d'armée* effected their retreat between the northern main road, on which the allies were advancing, and that followed by the left wing of their army. Although there are no main roads on this line from west to east, there are plenty of scarcely inferior ones leading to the Chiese; and on the 15th five Austrian *corps d'armée* were concentrated behind this river on the outskirts of the Mincio hills, two of them at Montechiaro, one at Lonato, one at Castiglione, and one at Castel Goffredo; while the remaining four corps, among them the two which had retreated along the Po, were concentrating in and about Mantua. The same day the Sardinians arrived in the neighbourhood of Brescia, where Garibaldi had preceded them. The latter, taking the hill road from Brescia, went with part of his troops to construct a bridge over the Chiese at Molinetto, while another small detachment was sent on the road to Lonato, to protect the flank of the 1st column. The detachment advancing on the road to Lonato fell in with some troops of General Urban at Treponti, near Rezzato, and had a sharp engagement with them, being forced to retire before overpowering numbers. At the report of this fight the 4th Sardinian division Cialdini was sent in advance of Brescia, but too late to take any part in the action.

The next day the French headquarters, as well as the mass of the army, arrived at the Mella, and the same day (the 16th) the Austrians abandoned their positions near the Chiese, evacuated Lonato, Montechiaro, and Castiglione, and withdrew towards the Mincio, General Gyulai's headquarters being transferred to Volta.

On the 17th Brescia was festively decorated, and resounding with cries of joy; for King Victor Emmanuel was making his entry, and the Sardinians passed through to take up a position in advance of Brescia. The Austrians, who had the day before evacuated Montechiaro, Castiglione, and Lonato, again returned to these positions. At the same time news were received of one Austrian body having descended by the Stelvio pass to Bormio, and of another threatening to come down the valley of the Chiese. The news spoke only of small bodies of men, mostly volunteers; but as it was known that the Austrians had lately paid great attention to the communications from Tyrol to the Valtellina, it was thought necessary to send Garibaldi, who had in the mean time occupied Salo on the Lago di Garda, to Sondrio, and to push forward the Sardinian division Cialdini (4th) towards Salo, and into the valley of the Upper Chiese.

On the 18th the emperor made his entry into Brescia, it is scarcely necessary to say amid the general enthusiasm of this most patriotic of towns. The same day the 2nd and 1st corps passed the Mella, and, without entering Brescia, took up a position before that town, and pushed their vanguard forward towards the plain of Montechiaro, while the Sardinians, still keeping a little in front, advanced their outposts to the Chiese, in the direction of Lonato.

On the 19th the 4th and 3rd French corps, which, it will be remembered, formed the right wing, and were following *en échelon*, likewise crossed the Mella, but lower down. Thus the whole army was fairly out in the plain. This repassing of the right wing was thought necessary to guard against any offensive return of the Austrians from the south.

On the 20th the Austrians a second time abandoned Castiglione and Montechiaro, retiring definitively over the Mincio, and leaving only two small corps in front of Peschiera. At the same time the last troops which retired on the Mantua road crossed the Oglio at Bozzolo, and burned down the bridge at that place as well as at Canneto.

At Montechiaro they left behind some of their own wounded, as well as those from Garibaldi's corps who had fallen into their hands in the skirmish of the 15th. This desertion of their wounded after evacuating a place was a general practice of the Austrians during the campaign in Italy. An army in retreat is often driven to adopt this expedient; and one could scarcely reproach the Austrians for doing so, were it not for the fact that, while they thus left their sick and wounded behind to the tender mercies of the allies, they represented the latter to their soldiers as *Thugs* and *Anthropophagi*, who killed their prisoners and wounded. This did not prevent the allies from making thousands of prisoners; but however obtuse the understanding of an Austrian soldier may be thought, he could not but see the contradiction between the words and deeds of his superiors, and towards the end believed the latter far more than the former.

In consequence of this retreat of the Austrians, a general advance took place all along the line on the following day, the 21st. The Sardinians, crossing the Chiese both at San Marco and Calcinatello, occupied Lonato, and pushed their *avant-garde* as far as Desenzano. The king himself transferred his headquarters to Calcinato. The 2nd and 1st French corps crossed likewise the Chiese at Montechiaro, and pushed their advanced guard to Castiglione and Esenta, on the outskirts of the Mincio hills; the 4th corps advanced towards the Chiese at Mezzano, and the 3rd followed an *étage* further back in its wake. The infantry of the guard followed general headquarters to Castenedolo, at the entrance of the plain of Montechiaro, and the cavalry of the guard encamped the same day in the plain itself.

On the 22nd, another short advance was made, the 1st and 2nd French corps occupied Castiglione and Esenta, the 4th corps advanced across the Chiese to Carpenedolo, the 3rd took its place at Mezzano, and general headquarters, together with the infantry of the guard, moved to Montechiaro.

Thus the allied army, with the exception of the 3rd French corps (Canrobert), which was at Mezzano, had crossed the Chiese, and was in position on the outskirts of the Mincio hills, forming a line from Desenzano by Lonato, Esenta, Castiglione, and Carpenedolo, being thus *á cheval* on both the great roads to the Mincio.

Slow as the advance had been from Milan to Brescia, it will be perceived that the march from Brescia was slower still. Besides the reasons before adduced, the difficulties of providing for the subsistence of so large an army, and the necessity of waiting for the siege train, there were other grounds which made caution advisable. The allies had arrived at the defensive positions of the Austrians, and every moment it might be expected to meet them in force. But more than anything else, the vacillation in the Austrian movements, the abandoning of Montechiaro and Castiglione, and the return again; the throwing-up of earthworks at Lonato and the abandonment of them, were calculated to cause some reflection: was it really indecision, or did it conceal some deep-laid scheme? According to all accounts brought on the 22nd, by people coming from the Mincio villages, there were only small bodies of the enemy on the west side of the Mincio. The Sardinians fell in with

189

a patrol sent by one of these, in the direction of Desenzano, the same morning but found nothing behind it.

Whether the emperor had information that something was preparing, or whether he was not quite decided what to do himself, it is a fact that, next day, headquarters were not moved as was expected, and the telegraph line which, according to his orders had been carried on to Lonato, was taken down and carried from Montechiaro to Castiglione. During the day, large columns of dust were observed in the direction of Mantua and the Goito road. A cavalry picket was sent in the plain towards Solferino, and fell in with some of the enemy's patrols, rather near to Castiglione; but, even with the best glass, nothing was seen at Solferino, which is visible from the hills near Castiglione. In the afternoon, the brothers Goddard tried from these hills a balloon ascent, on a larger scale than some days before from Castenedolo. On the Austrian side, where this ascent was seen, it is supposed that their plans were discovered by Messrs. Goddard. This remains to be proved, as well as whether the emperor had already, on the 23rd, any positive data about the movements of the Austrians. That something was suspected is certain; but the orders given out for the next day show that no general engagement was looked forward to, and that the movement of the allied armies was made with the view of seizing the dominating points of the Mincio hills.

The Sardinian army, which, having sent the division Cialdini to Salo, consisted only of four divisions, was to send one division in the direction of Peschiera, another in that of Pozzolengo, and a third towards Madonna della Scoperta. The first French corps (Baraguay d'Hilliers) was to march from Esenta on Solferino; the 2nd (MacMahon) from Castiglione on Cavriana; the 4th corps (Niel), strengthened by two divisions of cavalry, from Carpenedolo to Medole and Guidizzolo; the 3rd corps to advance from Mezzano to Medole; and the guard infantry, cavalry, and artillery, from Montechiaro and Castenedolo to Castiglione. A look at the map and a moment's reflection on these dispositions will show that they are an *ordre de marche* undertaken to secure the position of the Mincio hills and the road through the plain to Goito. The points to which the left wing and centre of the allies were directed are just about the middle of the Mincio range where it is highest, while the point which the right wing was to take covers a position in the plain. It was a movement with baggage, which surely would have been left behind had a battle been expected. Finally, the cavalry of the guard, which was still at Castenedolo at the entrance of the plain of Montechiaro, only had orders to start at nine a.m. and to take it easily, a disposition which cannot be understood, if one supposes that a battle was expected in the open Campo di Medole before Guidizzolo.

These considerations irresistibly lead to the conclusion that no general engagement was expected by the allies; there was no doubt a suspicion, but probably nothing beyond, until the sound of cannon at five a.m. announced—

CHAPTER 9

The Battle of Solferino

In order to give an idea how this battle, the greatest of modern times, after that of Leipsic, was brought about, it is necessary to cast a glance at the movements of the Austrians. Even now, when several months have passed, it is difficult to discover the real cause of uncertainty in the movements of the Austrian army. After crossing the Chiese on the 15th, it is in position at Lonato, Montechiaro, and Castiglione; on the 16th it retires towards the Mincio; on the 17th it is moved forward again; on the 20th it crossed the Mincio; and on the 23rd it returns and makes an offensive movement. On the 18th, it is true, General Gyulai is dismissed, and General Schlick takes the command of this the second army; but the change is merely nominal, for already, before the 15th, the emperor of Austria was at Verona, and had taken the supreme command of the army. Besides, this change of commanders falling just between the two changes of plans, has therefore probably no influence on either. It cannot be looked upon as a counter-manoeuvre against anything done by the allies, for all these latter did was what they had done all along—to advance in the track of the Austrians. The only admissible hypothesis, therefore, fully justified besides by history, is, that the Austrians did not exactly know what to do—whether to defend the Mincio line, or to retire into the vicinity of their strongholds.

They seemed, however, to have come to the conclusion that the system hitherto pursued in the direction of the campaign had led to a complete failure. The jealousy among the generals, each of whom thought himself the best qualified to command; the abnormal po-

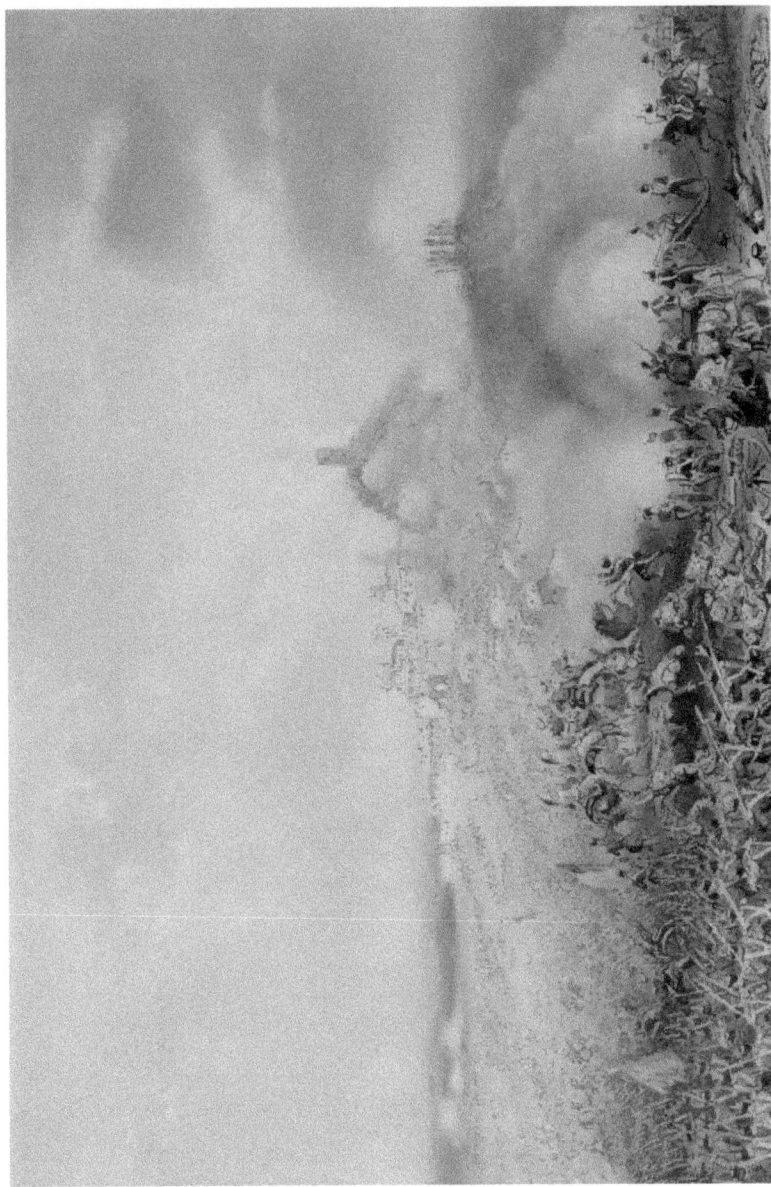

BATTLE OF SOLFERINO—ATTACK OF SOLFERINO BY THE FRENCH

sition of the chief of the staff, General Hess, as adviser, controller, and critic of the commander-in-chief; the old traditional system of directing operations from Vienna, rendered a hundred times more mischievous by the telegraph;—all these evils were expected to be remedied by the emperor's putting himself at the head of his army. At the same time the army was differently divided. When the advance into Piedmont took place, the first army, commanded by General Wimpfen, consisting of two and afterwards of three corps, the 6th, 10th, and 11th, remained as reserve in the Mincio; while the second army, commanded by General Gyulai, consisting of the 1st, 2nd, 3rd, 5th, 7th, 8th, and 9th corps, formed the active army. Both now coming into activity, they were more equally divided. General Gyulai, who had lost the confidence of the army, was removed, and Count Schlick appointed in his place. Many of the superannuated generals shared his fate, and were put on the retiring list. Finally, an acting quartermaster-general, General Kamming, was appointed, who, although nominally under General Hess, in reality filled his place.

All these changes being made, it was determined to take the offensive, and attack the allied armies in their positions on the western outskirts of the Mincio hills. For this purpose, the whole army received orders, in the evening of the 22nd, to recross the Mincio on the next morning. The four points chosen for crossing were Monzambano, Valeggio, Goito, and Mantua, the first two being used for the second army under General Schlick, and the two last for the first army, under Wimpfen. Of the former, the 8th corps (Benedeck), coming from Monzambano, occupied Pozzolengo; the 5th (Stadion), crossing at Valeggio, marched to Solferino, the 1st to Cavriana, and the 7th took position in the plain, between San Cassiano and Volta. Of the second army, the 3rd (Schwarzenberg) and the 9th (Schaffgotsch) went from Goito to Guidizzolo at the entrance of the plain of Medole; the 10th and the 11th took up a position to the left rear of them in the direction of Ceresara; and the 2nd (Lichstenstein), leaving Mantua by the gate of Pradella, went in the direction of the lower Oglio, and pushed forward its outposts to Acquanegra near the confluence of the Chiese and Oglio.

On the evening of the 23rd, these nine corps, numbering in all from 180,000 to 190,000 men, were in the positions assigned them; that is, the whole active Austrian army was encamped in a line from Pozzolengo to the lower Oglio, the length of which was quite twenty miles as the crow flies. Opposite to it was the allied army, extending from Lonato by Castiglione to Carpinedolo; that is on a line of about seven miles, with its reserves at Montechiaro and Castenedolo, and in a strength of from 140,000 to 150,000 men. Both had orders to advance the next day. The true intentions of the Austrians, however good, must remain a mystery, as they were never carried into effect: still, from their preparatory movements, it may be conjectured that they had conceived the grand idea which, as Sir William Napier tells us, was in great favour with the Spanish national forces in the Peninsular War, namely, of surrounding the enemy by a flanking movement, cutting him off from his line of operation, and crushing him between the lake and the Chiese. For this purpose the long line was next day to be drawn together on the left, and thus a large net prepared, in which the allies were to be caught. The 2nd corps, forming the extreme left was to move up the Oglio and Chiese, to Asola and Acqua Fredda, the 10th and 11th to Castel Goffredo, the 9th to Medole, and the rest to their front, all having the direction of Castiglione and Lonato. The three corps to the left, intrusted with the drawing together of the net, were to have the start, and to have completed their movements by nine a.m., when the emperor of Austria was to give the order for the general advance of the army.

Nothing could be bolder, to say the least, than this tactical combination for annihilating the enemy; and well might it have led the Austrian officers in their dreams to Brescia and Milan. Everyone knows that nothing is more fatal for a beaten army than to be enveloped on the battlefield—it is sure destruction. But like every other high game, it is not without its risks. A commander must feel very sure of beating the enemy, and be equally sure that he has *the time* necessary for carrying out his design, else he risks having his own army cut in two. That the Austrians, after Magenta and their retreat to the Mincio, had still such confidence in their success, shows they had a better opinion of themselves than others had; that the Austrians hoped to have time to execute their great circular movement, indicated that they had a worse opinion of their adversaries than the world in general entertained of them. Such were the hopes of the Austrians on the evening of the 23rd of June. Let us now see what their real position was. The long line which they occupied was about one-fourth in the Mincio hills, and three-fourths in the plain which extends from their southern outskirts towards the lower Oglio and the Po.

The Mincio, issuing from the Lago di Garda, runs due south, while the direction of the hills on both banks runs at right angles almost towards it; those on the right bank, with which alone we have to deal here, coming down from the north and north-west, strike the Mincio in a south-easterly direction. The hilly country, on the right bank of the Mincio, thus forms a tolerably regular parallelogram from north-west to south-east, the four angles of which are Lonato, Peschiera, Volta, and Castiglione. This parallelogram of hills is about twelve miles in length, and eight in width, and is divided longitudinally by the Redone, a little stream coming out of the hills between Lonato and Castiglione and running into the Mincio.

The hills rise gradually from the shores of the lake in successive irregular wave lines, the last toward the plain towering high above the rest, and forming, as it were, a mighty wall round the western and southern sides of the parallelogram. The southern side, above all, is remarkable for its height and steepness all along its length from Castiglione to Volta. Being formed of a succession of long, steep ridges, strongly indentated, it looks from the plain like the ruins of some Titanic stronghold destroyed by time, and overgrown with grass. Two points, higher than the rest, stand like keeps in the centre of this line of ridges. These two points are Solferino and Cavriana. Both detached from the others, and sloping down precipitously towards the plain, they resemble two bastions, while the lower, but scarcely less precipitous, slopes of San Cassiano, between them, may well represent the curtain of these gigantic bastions.

From the interior, another range of hills runs down towards this outer one. It skirts the northern or right bank of the little stream Redone, and comes down with it from the neighbourhood of Lonato, in an almost southerly direction, to within a mile from the heights of Solferino. It there makes a sudden bend to the north-east, runs on for a couple of miles in this direction, and then breaks off. At the point where it breaks off lies Pozzolengo, and at the point where the ridge approaches nearest to Solferino, stands, in an isolated position, the church of Madonna della Scoperta. Solferino and Cavriana on the outer ridge, and Pozzolengo and Madonna della Scoperta on the inner ridge, mark the position of the Austrians in the Mincio hills. The relative positions of these four points is such that if a line was drawn round them, it would give the figure of a truncated cone; Cavriana and Pozzolengo forming the base of it towards the Mincio, and Solferino and Madonna della Scoperta the top towards Castiglione and Lonato. With the exception of the road near the lake to Peschiera, the others leading through this hilly country to the Mincio all touch one or more of these four points; consequently, their possession shuts the hills of the Mincio to an advancing army.

While they thus in their ensemble give the command of the Mincio hills, each of these four points is an independent position in itself. Far above all the hills in their neighbourhood, each of them forms the centre of a group of ridges branching out from that centre. The position of the Austrians in the hills must thus be represented as a colossal natural redoubt, with four bastions, each of them with numerous outworks, and only assailable at the angles,— Solferino, Cavriana, Madonna della Scoperta, and Pozzolengo. The Austrians had four *corps d'armée* in this position, in all about 90,000 men. The 8th corps (Benedeck), forming the extreme right, held the points on the inner ridge, Pozzolengo and Madonna della Scoperta, making front against Lonato and the forces coming from that side. The 1st, 5th, and 7th corps held the outer ridge towards the plain and Castiglione, occupying Solferino, Cavriana, and San Cassiano lying between the two. This strong force, about 60,000 men, showed that the Austrians well knew the value of the position; for, being the strongest in the whole hill country, besides commanding two of the chief passages by Volta and Goito, it is the key to the Mincio, and while in the hands of the enemy no army can pass by.

Of the other five Austrian corps scattered in the plain, only two, namely, the 3rd and 9th, held what might be called a military position. They were at Guidizzolo, *à cheval* on the main-road from

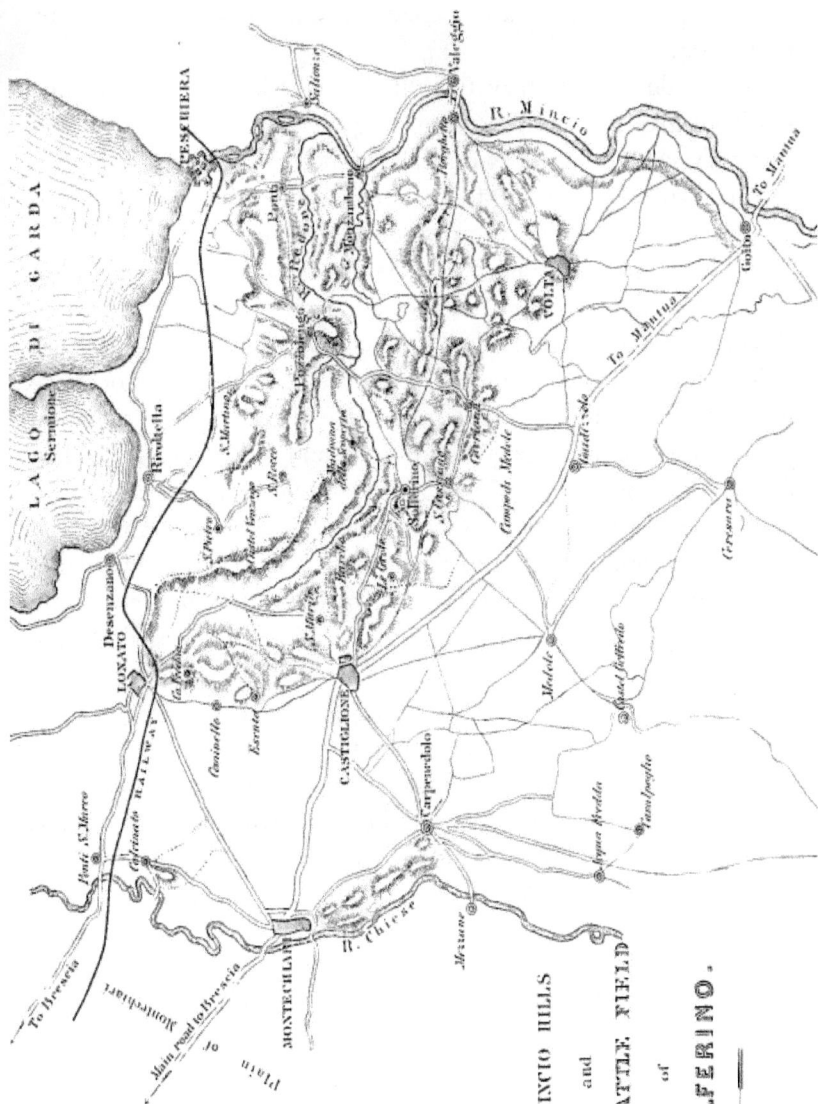

THE MINCIO HILLS
and
THE BATTLE FIELD
of
SOLFERINO.

Castiglione, thus guarding this road in front, as Cavriana and Solferino did from the flank. The three other *corps d'armée*, or about 60,000 men, were destined for the great flanking movement, and can therefore not be reckoned as forming part of the Austrian army in position.

The order of march of the allied armies for the 24th of June has been given in the preceding chapter. From it it will be seen that they were directed against all the points of the Austrian positions: naturally enough, for the possession of these points was absolutely necessary for the passage of the Mincio.

The left wing, formed by the Sardinian army, was directed on Pozzolengo and Madonna della Scoperta, the two keys of the inner ridge; the centre, composed of the 1st and 2nd French corps, with infantry of the Imperial Guard as reserve, had the task of occupying Solferino and Cavriana respectively,—that is, the commanding points in the outer ridge; while the 4th and 3rd French corps had to gain the main road to Goito at Guidizzolo. With the large plain and Mantua to the right, it was necessary to guard against any flank movement which the enemy might make, and this forced the allies to extend their right wing. In order to fill up the gap thus made between the latter and the centre, two divisions of cavalry were sent on the main road from Castiglione to Goito.

There were thus three distinct operations with three distinct objects. They reacted on each other, but they formed during the greater part of the day three distinct battles. The attack on the centre, being directed against the real key of the whole position, was the most important, because it decided the success of the rest.

From whichever side the traveller approaches the Mincio hills, one of the first objects which will attract his attention is a square weather-beaten tower on a high conical hill, covered with green turf. It is the *Spia d'Italia*, so called because from it the eye can pry over a large part of the Lombard plain, over the shores of the Lago di Garda, and over the Mincio, far beyond the spires and domes of Mantua. The hill on which it is built, called the *Bocca* di Solferino, rises abruptly to the north-west of the village to which it has given its name. After attaining two-thirds of its height, it throws out two spurs, like two horns, one to its left—sharp, narrow, precipitous, showing a bold outline towards the plain, and falling off suddenly. It is called Monte di Cipressi, from a row of these trees which crown its summit, conspicuous from afar. The other to the right, having no particular name, but commonly called Monte della Chiesa, from the church of San Nicholas on the top. Stretching out in the direction of Castiglione, it rises abruptly above the valley of the Redone, and throws out towards this river a lower, but equally abrupt branch, similarly crowned on its summit with a church—that of San Pietro. On the other side—that is, towards the plain—it slopes down more gradually towards the Monte di Cipressi. In the hollow between the two lies the little hamlet of Pozzo di Solferino, as the villagers, and Pozzo Catena, as the maps call it. The spurs, although forming part of the group of the Bocca, are separated by a depression in the ground from the Bocca itself; and this depression has been used to lead the roads from Castiglione over the group to the village of Solferino behind it. There are two of these roads,—one, which runs along the plain at the base of the hills, and leaving the village of Grole to its left, turns up between the Monte di Cipressi and the Monte della Chiesa to the hamlet of Pozzo Catena, and crosses the ridge between the Bocca di Solferino and the Monte della Chiesa; the other, leaving Castiglione and the outer ridge to its right, winds along the hills almost parallel to the former, and rising in a steep incline between Monte della Chiesa and the smaller spurs of San Pietro, thrown out by the latter, tops the ridge at the same point as the road through the plain. Both roads united there, run down to the village of Solferino. Just where the two unite rise the walls of the church St. Nicholas, occupying the whole summit of the Bocca. These walls, about 20 to 30 feet high, inclose besides the church, a belfry, the schools, and the dwelling of the parish priest, which occupy three sides. In front of the church is a large open plot of ground, and to the right of it the hill, protected only by a low wall, descends abruptly towards the hill road, which runs up at its foot. Beyond the walls of St. Nicholas, the summit of the Bocca presents a narrow green plateau, with another much whiter-looking enclosure at its edge. This is the cemetery of Solferino. Beyond the cemetery, but separated from it by a considerable depression in the ground, begin the *Scale* or ladders of Solferino, a succession of steep, precipitous ridges between the plain and the valley of the Redone, which extend as far as the little village of Grole.

The hill group of Solferino forms, then, a succession of formidable positions, easy to defend and very difficult to approach. In the two roads are deep and narrow defiles, flanked by the spurs between which they run up to the top of the ridge. By the ridge itself the advance is scarcely less dangerous, for each ridge is commanded by the following one. Besides this, each is likewise separated from the other by a strong depression in the ground, forming, as it were, the ditch to each of these successive positions.

While the position of Solferino is thus well protected in front and in the flanks, it is not less so in the rear; for, from the foot almost of the Bocca hill rises another ridge, sloping down in terrace-like plateaux towards the scattered houses of the village of San Cassiano in the plain; between this ridge and the base of the Bocca hill the road from San Cassiano to the village of Solferino runs up. While the slopes of San Cassiano are held, it is, therefore, like the roads in front, a defile. The ridge of San Cassiano extends, in an almost uninterrupted line, to Cavriana, the sister group of Solferino, which had been chosen by the Austrian s for their reserves.

Of a similar conformation as Solferino, the slopes of San Cassiano are to it what the Scale are to Solferino—a kind of natural outwork. Both look down on what is called the Campo di Medole, an open plain devoid of trees, through which the main road from Castiglione passes to Goito. This road, coming out of Castiglione to the left of the Mincio hills, runs for about half a mile through a country like the rest of Upper Lombardy, covered with vineyards and mulberry-trees, but less cut up by canals than other portions of it. There being a scantiness of water, the vegetation is not very rich, and the ground more open and adapted to military movements. After running through this country for a mile and a half, the road enters the Campo di Medole just at the point where a cross road intersecting the plain runs in a straight line to Medole. The main road continues for about two miles and a half in this open plain, until it comes to the outskirts of the village of Guidizzolo, where the trees begin again. The open *campo*, thus intersected by the main road, covers a space of two and a half square miles between the points San Cassiano, Cavriana, Guidizzolo, Robecco, and Pieve. It is scantily cultivated, with only here and there a corn or maize field, and the rest bad pasture-ground.

About a mile from the southern outskirts of Campo di Medole runs the road from Medole to Guidizzolo, and parallel almost to the main road to Goito, another from Carpinedolo by Medole to Ceresara, in the direction of Mantua. The Austrians with two corps, the 3rd and 9th, at Guidizzolo and Medole, and with the 11th corps at Ceresara, had the command of the main road, as well as the roads passing through Medole.

Such was the Austrian position on the morning of St. John's day, 1859.

Partly to escape the heat, and partly to conceal the movements of their army, the allies had been in the habit of stirring very early. On the 24th then the general order of march was for three o'clock in the morning.

The 1st French corps, which was encamped at Esenta, started somewhat earlier, so as to be in line with the others. The three divisions of this corps were divided into two columns; one division (Ladmirault) was sent by the hill road towards Solferino, while the two others (Forey and Bazaine) with artillery and baggage, followed the road by the plain.

This latter column had scarcely left Castiglione, when it met the outposts of the Austrians at the little hamlet Le Fontane, lying in a hollow between two spurs of the first range of heights beyond Castiglione, called Monte di Valcura. This hamlet is not less than three miles from Solferino. The Austrian outposts fell back to the village of Grole, which lies in a narrow valley formed by the heights of Valcura and the Scale di Solferino. This village, more than a mile in front of Solferino, the Austrians evidently considered as part of their position, for they stood, and it required some effort to drive them out. By the time the village of Grole had been taken—that is, about six a.m.—the division Ladmirault, which was following the mountain road, came up in line with the column which had taken the village of Grole.

From this point the two columns advanced in parallel directions on Solferino. The left divided itself into three columns, and began to climb up the Scale di Solferino, which, as it will be remembered, extend to the village of Grole, while the right column attacked the Monte Feline. Monte Feline is one of the many detached hills which are scattered about at the foot of the heights all along from

Castiglione to Cavriana and Volta. These detached hills were of considerable service in the attack of both Solferino and Cavriana,—they became positions for the artillery of the allies, and afforded a shelter behind which they could form their columns of attack.

While the two columns of the 1st corps thus advanced, the 2nd corps (MacMahon), had debouched from Castiglione by the main road to Goito. It was to proceed on this road as far as the entrance of the Campo di Medole, where the cross road runs from San Cassiano to Medole. Here it was to turn off towards San Cassiano and Cavriana. Long before it reached this point it found, at five a.m. the enemy before it at a farmhouse to the left of the main road, called Casa Morino. The sound of cannon and musketry which came over from the left, announced that the 1st corps was already engaged. At the same time large masses of troops were observable on the slopes of San Cassiano, moving towards Solferino. Both these were sufficient reasons for advancing, and thus relieving the 1st corps; but the 2nd corps had to form the link between the centre and the right wing of the allied armies, it could not therefore leave the main road and march on San Cassiano, until the 4th corps had likewise debouched from Medole into the open Campo di Medole, lest the Austrians should throw themselves in the gap thus left between the centre and the right wing; and there was no trace of the 4th corps. It had not arrived at Medole: but had already found the outposts of the Austrians a mile or so before it, and had engaged them. They withdrew to the village of Medole, which they occupied in strength. The division Luzy succeeded, after a hard struggle, in dislodging them, and in taking two guns, besides a number of prisoners; they belonged to the 9th Austrian corps, which, coming from Guidizzolo, had occupied Medole the same morning. They retired towards Robecco, a little village between Medole and Guidizzolo; while one brigade of the 4th corps pursued this body, another brigade was sent on to the road to Ceresara, where the 11th Austrian corps began to show; at the same time the artillery was sent by the cross road which leads through the Campo di Medole to San Cassiano, and tried to take up a position at the entrance of this open plain, supported by the division Vinoy.

While this passed on the right wing, MacMahon waited with

impatience for the debouching of the 4th corps in the plain, in order to begin his own movement on Cavriana, which was so much the more necessary as the battle towards Solferino seemed to assume greater and greater proportions. He sent repeatedly messages to General Niel, commanding the 4th corps, to press on him the necessity of attacking the enemy, who seemed disposed to make an offensive movement between the 2nd and the 4th corps; the answer was, that he would come out into the plain as soon as he had taken Medole, but that he could not join before the 3rd corps was united to him on his own right.

At half past eight o'clock, the Austrians showing a disposition to make an offensive movement, the 2nd corps drove the enemy's outposts from the farm Casa Morino, and took up a position before this farm, perpendicularly to the road to Goito, occupying both sides of it, so as to extend its right in the direction of Medole, towards the 4th corps. The ground thus occupied was not yet out in the open plain, but among the vineyards and mulberry-trees, which extend on both sides of the Goito road, as far as the entrance of the Campo di Medole.

Up to that moment, that is, about nine o'clock, the French had had all the attacking to themselves, now the Austrians began to take the offensive in two directions—Guidizzolo by the main road, against the 2nd corps (MacMahon), and from Guidizzolo, likewise, towards Medole.

A heavy column of Austrians coming from Guidizzolo advanced against the line formed by the 2nd corps; a numerous artillery guarded it, which took up a position in the plain, and opened fire on MacMahon's corps. The four batteries belonging to this *corps d'armée* were advanced, and began to reply. It was the first time during the campaign that the rifled gun had a regular encounter with the old model gun of the Austrians, for at Magenta the Austrians were too timid to expose their cannon to the risk of being taken; and, after a very short trial, the superiority of the rifled cannon was established. Several ammunition-waggons were blown up, and the Austrian artillery was just retiring, when the two French cavalry divisions arrived, at the rear of the 2nd corps. Their horse artillery was immediately sent to the right of the line, in the direction of Medole, and opened up on the left flank of the

Austrians, while the batteries of the 2nd corps played upon them in front; taken thus in front and flank, the Austrians found their position in the open plain untenable. It was on this occasion that a brigade of Austrian cavalry (Mensdorff) boldly advanced to draw the fire of the French artillery upon it, and thus to extricate the Austrian artillery from the awkward position into which it had got. Certainly they did attract the fire of the French artillery, for the line occupied by them could be traced by the carcasses of horses and corpses of men. Some French *chasseurs* who were posted on the line occupied by the 2nd corps were sent forward, and the two bodies met. The French believe that they inflicted great loss on the Austrians, the latter maintain the reverse; a simple spectator could not decide in the cloud of dust; which version is the true one, but he could see that the Austrian hussars got near the square formed on the extreme left, by the 11th Chasseurs-à-Pied, and the 72nd of the line, and were soon after riding back over the plain in thin and scattered ranks. But the diversion had accomplished its object, although at a heavy loss, and the Austrian artillery had time to retire out of the plain, in the direction of Guidizzolo. The plain became thus, as it were, a kind of neutral ground, across which the 3rd Austrian and 2nd French corps sent their shot and shell. It remained so during the greater part of the day, for when the 2nd French corps advanced towards San Cassiano, the reserve artillery under General Soleil, coming out from Medole, took up the game of balls on the other side; and certainly in this artillery duel the French rifled gun had all the advantage. Gun after gun and battery after battery did the Austrians bring to the outskirts of the plain, only to be taken back disabled, after firing a few shots, which fell short.

The sound of the cannon carried the news of the battle to the emperor at Montechiaro, just about the time when a letter from Mantua informed him of the plan of the Austrians directed against his right flank. The intelligence was by no means reassuring, for it prevented the possibility of weakening the right flank just at the moment when the Austrian advance by the main road from Goito made it necessary to fill the gap left between the centre and right wing of the allied armies.

As a general battle seemed impending, the first thing was to bring up the reserves. The infantry of the guard, who had already

BATTLE OF SOLFERINO—ATTACK OF CAVRIANA BY THE FRENCH

started from Montechiaro, received orders to accelerate its march, and to debouch on the road from Castiglione to Goito, while the cavalry and reserve artillery was ordered to start immediately from Carpenedolo, and come up behind the 2nd corps. Thus the first danger from this side was parried; the infantry ready to receive the enemy, should he succeed in making a gap between the centre and right wing, and disposable for Solferino when the cavalry would come up.

The emperor mounted on horseback, and proceeded by the road from Castiglione to the 2nd corps, occupying at that moment the most exposed position. Having observed the state of things from Monte Medolano, near the Casa Morino, he saw that nothing could be done until the 4th corps on the right could debouch in the plain towards Guidizzolo, and thus effect its junction with the centre. Orders were consequently despatched to General Neil to make every effort in that direction, and to Marshal Canrobert, who was following with the 3rd corps on the extreme right, to support as much as possible the movement of the 4th corps on Guidizzolo; but he was warned, at the same time, of the flanking columns which the Austrians intended to send from Mantua to turn his right. These dispositions being made, the emperor went to the 1st corps, which was advancing on Solferino.

Whether the emperor had formed his plan from the nature of the position before coming to the battlefield, or whether this plan was inspired by the aspect of the position from Monte Medolano, it is, of course, impossible to say; but so much is certain, that already at Monte Medolano the plan seems to have assumed a definite shape; for in the orders sent to the 4th corps, Cavriana was given as its object, after taking Guidizzolo, clearly indicating that it was already seen that Solferino and Cavriana were the keys of the position, and that the effort must be made in the centre to cut in two the long line of the Austrians.

While these things were going on, the 1st corps was gradually advancing in the direction of Solferino. The first division (Forey), which had succeeded in getting possession of Monte Feline, was detached along the main ridge, in the direction where the road from the plain winds up its way between the Scale and Monte di Cipressi, and had established a battery on that point against the Austrian artillery, which had taken its position partly on the Monte di Cipressi, and round the base of the square tower on the Bocca di Solferino. Protected by the battery, the brigade Dieu first advanced up to the base of the Monte di Cipressi and the Bocca, but was stopped there by the cross fire which was brought to bear upon it from both those points. The 2nd division of this corps (Ladmirault) had likewise succeeded in gaining the first heights of the Scale di Solferino, and advanced step by step higher and higher; but the nearer it came to Solferino the greater became the difficulty; and after a two hours' struggle in the heat of the sun and under the fire of the Austrians, which became more and more intense, the division was exhausted; it had suffered great losses, and it became necessary to support it with the 3rd division of the corps (Bazaine), which had been, until then, kept back in reserve. The 1st Zouaves and the 34th of the line were sent forward, and brought new life into the attack, and with their assistance the column was able to make its way to the point where the Scala joins the edge of the Monte della Chiesa. The crest of the Scala ridge contracts as it approaches this point, until it is no more than about a hundred yards broad. It falls off precipitously to the left, looking down into the valley of the Redone, while on the right it slopes down more gently towards the hamlet Pozzo Catena. The whole of this slope is closely planted with vines and mulberries. Just at the outskirts of the Monte della Chiesa is the cemetery, occupying the whole breadth of the crest. This cemetery had been loopholed all round, and was strongly occupied by the Austrians, and this had to be taken; for on one side, towards the valley of the Redone, there was no passage, the ground falling off suddenly, and on the other was the slope, which was flanked not only by the cemetery, but likewise from the northern side of the Monte di Cipressi turned towards Pozzo Catena, and the Bocca itself; besides which, it was commanded by the higher part of the Monte della Chiesa in front. One attempt after another was made by the Zouaves and soldiers of the line to drive the Austrians from the cemetery; they failed. The French had to fall back, and even defend themselves against several attacks which the Austrians made from the neighbourhood of the cemetery.

Such was the state of affairs on this point when the emperor arrived between nine and ten a.m. Both columns had advanced to the foot of the real position of Solferino, but had there come to a stop. The 2nd division (Ladmirault) was well-nigh used up; the 3rd had likewise all its troops, except one regiment, engaged, and the 1st corps had only its 2nd brigade more or less intact.

On arriving, the emperor ascended Monte Feline, where one battery of the 1st division was in position. It was evident, at whichever side the attack succeeded, the other position of the enemy must fail. If the Monte di Cipressi was taken and the Bocca, that is one spur, and the nucleus of the position on the other spur, the Monte della Chiesa and the cemetery were outflanked; while if the attack succeeded on this latter point, the same happened to the Monte di Cipressi and the Bocca di Solferino. In this respect, therefore, the Austrians were quite right in assuming the position of Solferino; for they held *both*, and the two defended each other most effectually. That the French ultimately did take both, seems therefore not so much the fault of the positions as of the Austrians.

As far as the ground itself was concerned, the Monte della Chiesa was easier to take, for it was only slightly elevated above the Scale at their junction with it; but its position forming the extreme point of a semicircle of heights occupied by Austrian infantry and artillery, it was more exposed to flanking fire than the Bocca and the Monte di Cipressi on their southern slopes towards the plain, where the 1st division of Marshal Baraguay d'Hilliers was advancing. But the ground itself on this point was far more difficult, for both the Bocca and the Monte di Cipressi present from the plain the appearance of one of the grassy mountains of Radnorshire, rising up abruptly to a height of 200 feet, and separated from all the lower heights in front of them by a corresponding depression in the ground. It is this very steepness which makes the fire from above less dangerous to a column which has reached the foot of them.

In this perplexing position, the emperor determined to try and penetrate by the road which leads up to the hamlet of Pozzo Catena, between the Scale held by the 2nd and 3rd divisions and the Monte di Cipressi. For this purpose, the only remaining brigade (D'Alton) of the 1st corps, with four pieces of the reserve artillery of the same corps was formed in columns of attack, and, General Forey placing himself at its head, advanced through the vineyards which cover both sides of the road.

The column made its way successfully to the entrance of the hamlet, which the Austrians had barricaded. But at this entrance there are garden-walls on both sides, which had been loopholed, and were held in force. At the same time, the column was taken by the Austrians in its right flank from the edge and sides of the Monte di Cipressi, and so ill-treated that it had to turn back, General Forey himself having been wounded.

This was the crisis of the battle. Evidently Solferino was the key of the Austrian position and of the Mincio hills. Upon its possession depended the fate of the day; if the French succeeded in taking it, they had broken through the Austrian centre, and at the same time defeated their ambitious flank movement, which was based on the possession of the hills. If they failed, nay, even if they allowed the Austrians to retain it much longer, there was every chance of the enemy being able to complete this movement to the right flank of the allies, and come down with four corps on the two which formed their right wing.

The 1st corps was completely used up, having only one regiment left which had not been engaged; all the rest had suffered severely. The 3rd and 4th corps had enough to do on the right, and might have perhaps more to do than they could manage if the four Austrian corps came up; the 2nd corps could not be moved, because the 4th on its right had not yet approached, and the cavalry of the Imperial Guard had not come up from Castenedolo to fill up the gap which the approach of the 2nd corps to Solferino would have caused. Besides, the 2nd corps had likewise to keep in check the enemy's forces at San Cassiano, which might otherwise have fallen upon the right flank of the allies. There remained, the Piedmontese as the left wing, and the guards. A message was sent to the king, requesting him to send a division by Castel Venzago and Madonna della Scoperta towards Solferino, so as to help the attack in front. From the king the message soon came back that he had found the enemy in strength at San Martino and could not send assistance. Although the Austrians had given up their attack from the Campo di Medole against the 2nd corps, it was by no means certain that they would not return with renewed strength; still, as upon the taking of Solferino depended everything else, the infantry of the Imperial Guard was ordered to draw from Castiglione to the left, and come up to the rear of the 1st corps. It could thus be used as a support both to this and to the 2nd corps if required.

This was between eleven and twelve a.m. By the time the division Manèque, composed of the *voltigeurs* and the *chasseurs-à-pied*, had joined the rear of the 1st corps, the crisis had passed. The 4th corps, which had been impatiently waited for, at last debouched on the outskirts of the Campo di Medole, placed its whole artillery (forty-two guns) in position, and General Neil sent word that he was able to move on Cavriana. There seemed consequently no danger from the left, at any rate, for the moment, and the guard could be employed in the mean time to take Solferino.

Neither had the Austrians lost their time on this point. Well aware of the importance of the position, they had brought up their 1st corps from Cavriana to support the 3rd, which had been considerably shaken by the French attack. It placed itself side by side with the corps, which had until then repelled the attack, and it was to the united efforts of the two that the corps of Baraguay d'Hilliers had to yield.

When the Garde Impériale had come up, no time was lost in organizing a combined attack with all the forces; the 3rd division of the 1st corps was ordered forward against the cemetery, the 1st division was sent in two columns against the hamlet, and the *chasseurs-à-pied* and 1st and 2nd Voltigeurs directed against the Bocca and the Monte di Cipressi, the 2nd brigade and the grenadiers remaining in reserve. To support this movement the artillery of the guard was sent forward, and having taken up a position a few hundred yards from the heights occupied by the Austrians, they opened fire upon them from the plain, while the whole artillery of the 1st corps, partly from Monte Feline and partly from the Scale directed their fire likewise on the semicircle occupied by the Austrians. It was magnificent to hear these sixty guns all directing their fire on an area of scarce one-third of a square mile, thundering away, and filling the air with their shells. They had not been long at work, when the fire of the Austrians slackened, and then the columns advanced. The *chasseurs-à-pied* and the *voltigeurs* of the guard reached the foot of the Bocca and Monte di Cipressi at a run. The next moment their knapsacks were on the ground, the cry of *Vive l'Empereur* resounded in the air, and the chasseurs and *voltigeurs* were swarming up the steep sides of the Bocca and the Monte di Cipressi with an agility truly admirable. Whether it was this almost superhuman feat, on a hot afternoon in June, or whether the fire of the artillery had demoralized the Austrians, at any rate the chasseurs and *voltigeurs* crowned the heights in a few minutes after they had started, taking eight guns.[1]

The division Forey about the same time penetrated into the hamlet, which had been barricaded, and most of the houses of which had been loopholed. Although by the taking of the Bocca this hamlet was outflanked, and the retreat cut off, the resistance was still considerable, especially in the first houses at the entrance. But it could but be desultory, for while the division Forey entered the village from the road and from the heights to the right, one brigade of the division Bazaine came down upon it from the slopes of the Scale on the left.

The cemetery was still held, as well as the church behind it. The 78th of the line was led against the former, which, deprived of its formidable protector, the cross-fire from the Bocca and the Cyprus Hill, was taken with little trouble. The troops which held the church behind surrendered to the *voltigeurs*.

This was a little past two p.m. Just about that time the arrival of the cavalry of the Imperial Guard allowed the 2nd corps (Mac-Mahon) to begin its forward movement on San Cassiano. This newly-arrived cavalry was placed to the left of the two divisions of cavalry, which had come up earlier in the day, with the order to form *en échelon*, and occupy the place which was to be left free by the advance of the 2nd corps. Thus all along the western outskirts of the Campo di Medole there was a long line of cavalry leaning with its right on the artillery of the 4th corps, and joining the 2nd corps with its left.

This latter had already moved its 1st division to the left in the direction of Solferino, and now the whole corps went on towards San Cassiano. The village itself, consisting of detached houses scattered about in the plain, affords no position, except in as far

1. M. Bossoli's sketch gives an excellent idea of the attack on the left, and in the centre. There is the cemetery, the Church of San Nicholas, the Spia, and to the right the Monte di Cipressi, and in the hollow the hamlet of Pozzo Catena or Pozzo di Solferino.

as the road from Solferino to Cavriana comes down through it; it was taken without much trouble by the Turcos and the 45th of the line; and the former advanced and took the first detached hill of the ridge which runs behind San Cassiano to Cavriana.

This advance in the direction of Cavriana told very much on the Austrian troops, who still tried to hold the hills behind Solferino; but it was evident that, if it was not checked, those troops would be cut off, and at the same time Cavriana and the passage of Valeggio. The loss of the position of Solferino had decided the day, and the Austrians from that moment began to fight for their retreat. It was still, however, not more than three p.m., there were more than five hours of daylight remaining; it was all-important, therefore, to keep the allies from Cavriana as long as possible, so as to gain time to effect the retreat.

In the plain this led to some pretty evolutions of cavalry on both sides, more interesting for the spectator than of any consequence for the fortune of the day. Seen from the hills, it looked more like show than business, although the riderless horses and dismounted men proved that it was not quite child's play.

But it was on the heights behind San Cassiano that the Austrians made their great effort to check the advance on Cavriana. The first detached hill of the range, where the Turcos had established themselves became the object of a sanguinary struggle. Taken and retaken three times, it was at last carried by a combined effort of the whole division De la Motterouge, supported by a brigade of the grenadiers of the guard, which had been sent up as reserve. The reason of this hard struggle was that the 2nd corps had orders to wait for the coming up, in line, of the 1st corps and the *voltigeurs*, who were to advance from Solferino on Cavriana, while the 2nd corps advanced from San Cassiano. With this order, the 2nd corps could never pursue the enemy whenever he was driven from the position, and thus he had time to re-form and try a new attack.

By half-past three p.m. the hills behind Solferino were clear of the Austrians, the main body of the defenders being thrown back on Cavriana, while their right wing was pressed towards its own right in the direction of Monzambano. The *voltigeurs* and brigade of grenadiers of the guard and 1st division of the 1st corps now came up in a line with the 2nd corps, which had just succeeded in retaking the detached hillock, for which it had been fighting more than an hour; and from this moment the fight in the centre looked very much like a game of chess, in which the emperor of the Freuch had the first move. As a sight, the advance on Cavriana was unique. Had it not been for the live shells and the poor fellows lying on the ground, it might have been thought a manoeuvring-ground, so regular were both the advance and retreat. About five p.m. the *voltigeurs* entered Cavriana from the hills, and the Turcos from the road below.

There were three hours more of daylight remaining, the enemy was in full retreat on his right, and in the centre all now depended on the taking of Guidizzolo, and thus cutting off the corps which had Mantua and Goito as their line of retreat. But, fortunately for the Austrians, the right wing of the allies had not been so successful as the centre. As will be remembered, the 4th corps was in possession of Medole by seven a.m., and had immediately advanced on Guidizzolo, where the 3rd and 9th Austrian corps were concentrated. The direct road from Medole to Guidizzolo passes through the village of Robecco, about three miles distant from the former; but there is likewise another road, which comes out into the Campo di Medole, and leads into the high road from Castiglione to Guidizzolo. It was on both these roads that the 4th corps tried to advance, but as it had likewise in the beginning to send a detachment to watch the road to Ceresara, it could not stir until the 3rd corps had time to occupy Medole, and thus protect the flank and rear of the 4th corps. The third corps having left Mezzano at three a.m., arrived at Castel Goffredo at seven a.m., and caught some Austrian lancers or hussars there. At nine a.m. it arrived at Medole, which was the point where it had to protect the right wing of the allied army. It relieved the 4th corps from guarding the road to Ceresara, and took up a position *en potence*, that is, bent back to its right. The 4th corps tried now to move on Guidizzolo. It succeeds in debouching on the plain, with the artillery, consisting of forty-two field-pieces, under the orders of General Soleil, and from this moment this side of the plain takes up the artillery duel which had been previously going on on the other side, where the 2nd corps was. But the infantry of the 4th corps could not get beyond Robecco on the right, the hamlet

Baete in the centre, and the Casa Nova to the left. Robecco is a little village on the road from Medole to Guidizzolo, not more than a mile distant from this latter; Baete, a hamlet on the road from Robecco into the plain; and Casa Nova, an isolated house near the high road to Guidizzolo. These three points, not a mile distant from each other, became from early morning the scene of a desperate struggle. They formed the line of defence of the Austrians in advance of Guidizzolo, and for six hours, from ten a.m. till three p.m., the 4th corps took and lost them again. During all this time General Niel addressed incessant demands to Marshal Canrobert, to send one or two of his divisions to Robecco, so as to allow the entire 4th corps to debouch into the plain, take Guidizzolo, and thus cut off the Austrian corps on their left. But Marshal Canrobert did not think it prudent too much to weaken the corps destined to check the attack, which it was known the Austrians intended to make on the right flank of the allies. And there were, indeed, in the earlier part of the day considerable columns seen moving to the right; they had even been fired upon by the artillery. But as nothing was now seen of these columns, and as the 4th corps, unable to advance, continued its demands for assistance, the marshal went himself to the spot about three p.m., and having seen the critical position of things, sent orders to the division Renaud, which was observing the road to Ceresara, to draw towards Robecco, and thus relieve the right of the 4th corps; at the same time the 1st brigade of the division Trochu was likewise, ordered up. This was about four p.m.; and while the artillery still continued its duel in the plain, General Luzy was sent with six battalions towards Guidizzolo. The column advanced up to the first houses of the village, but the troops, who had fought incessantly and without food for so many hours, were unable to penetrate or even keep their ground. General Niel, still intent on his purpose, and having obtained from Marshal Canrobert another division (Bourbatis), as reserve, sent General Trochu, with his division and the brigade Bataille, again on Guidizzolo. This was just about the time the centre of the allies entered Cavriana; and had the attack succeeded, the results can scarcely be calculated. The column had advanced half-way between Casa Nova and Guidizzolo, when a violent thunderstorm, which had been threatening for several hours, descended, thereby preventing all possibility of an attack. The artillery alone was not to be deterred by the clouds of dust and the violent showers which succeeded them, they kept up their fire during the greatest part of the time the storm lasted. It was not more than three-quarters of an hour; but they were a great gain; for the 4th corps, thoroughly exhausted, did not renew the attack on Guidizzolo, so the Austrians had full time to withdraw in that direction.

When the storm was over, the Austrians were seen retiring, partly in the plain between Cavriana and Volta, partly on the mountain road, but specially on the former; for the division Bazaine, of the 1st corps, having gained the direct road to Valeggio, the retreat was pressed towards the plain. While they were thus retreating, two batteries of horse artillery were brought up on Madonna delle Piere, a detached hill in front of Cavriana, where the emperor of Austria had stood not two hours before. They opened fire on the masses below, and changed a tolerably orderly retreat into a complete *sauve qui peut*. A couple of regiments of cavalry and a few guns might have driven the whole mass anywhere.

But whether the emperor had views of his own on the subject, or whether the troops were too exhausted, no effort was made to disturb the retreat, except on the road to Valeggio. As for the greater part of the army, it was no doubt impossible for them to make further exertions; they had been fighting in the sun ever since early in the morning; they had no regular meal, only a bit of bread or biscuit; it would have been almost too much to expect from human nature that it should still keep up; but there was more than half of the 3rd corps remaining, which had taken no part in the fatigues of the day; and there was the cavalry, which had not been overworked; and the greatest part of the reserve artillery.

In order to complete the narrative of the battle it is necessary to cast a glance at the left wing, composed of the Piedmontese army. Theirs was, as it were, the third battle of the 24th of June, and had less connection with the two already narrated than the latter have between themselves. In character it was the counterpart of the attack on the right wing by the 4th French corps—a sanguinary struggle for a few points taken and lost in turn, and finally decided by the success in the centre.

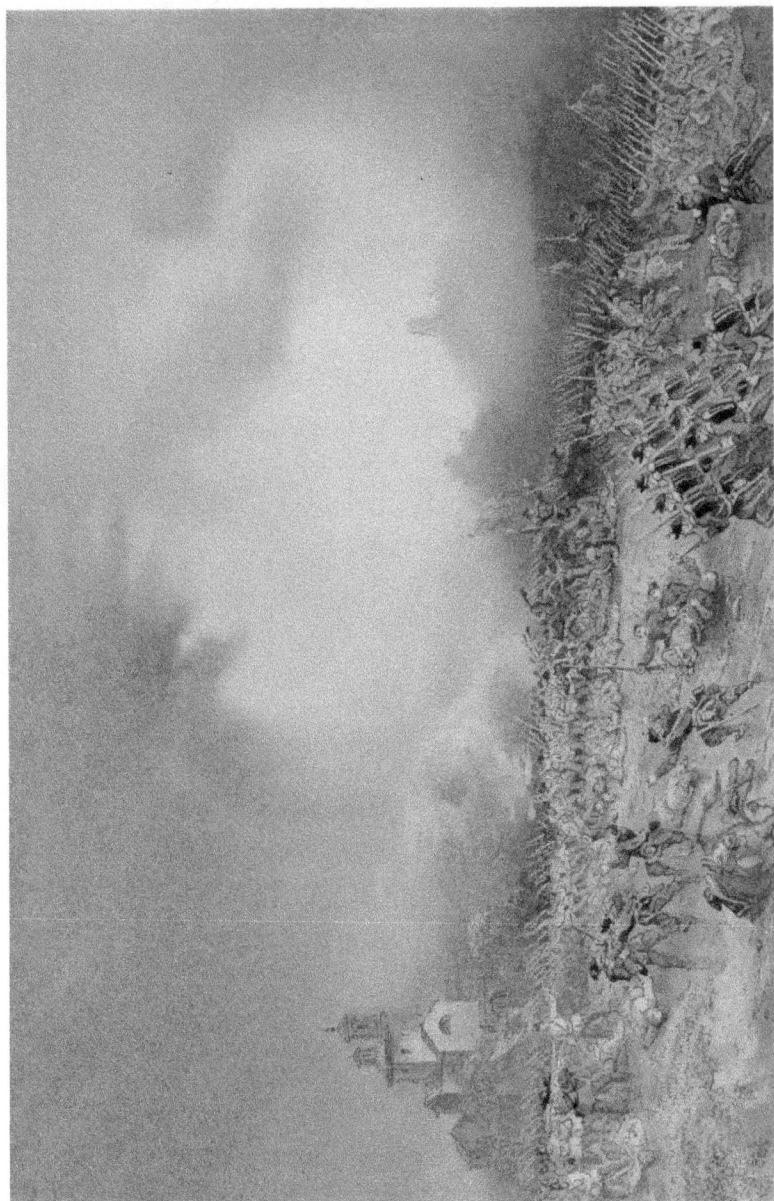

BATTLE IF SOLFERINO—ATTACK OF THE MADONNA DELLA SCOPERTA BY THE PIEDMONTESE

In the description of the Mincio hills, mention was made of an inner ridge of heights which rises on the north bank of the little stream Redone, and continues as far as Pozzolengo. They form a succession of plateaux abutting all on the two points of Pozzolengo and Madonna della Scoperta, which are, as it were, the backbone of these ribs. The direction of this backbone is from north-east to south-west, and the ribs fit in almost at right angles to it. The first and shortest of these are the heights of San Martino, in a line with the island of Sermione, in the Lago di Garda; they form the first group of heights rising up from the lake, and at their foot runs the railway, as well as the road from Desenzano to Pozzolengo. Intersecting each other just at that point, the group of San Martino is consequently of the greatest importance in the defence of this part of the Mincio hills. Like most of these hilly groups, it is a Solferino on a small scale, with a nucleus on which stands the church of San Martino, and with a number of spurs, almost every one of them with a *cascina*, or detached farmhouse, surrounded by trees, on the summit of it. Behind the group of San Martino come other ridges, each longer than the preceding one, the last forming almost an uninterrupted line from Lonato by Castel Venzago to Madonna della Scoperta.

According to the programme for St. John's day, the Piedmontese, who were occupying the hills before Lonato and the slopes of Desenzano, on the Lago di Garda, were to advance on Pozzolengo, while the centre of the army advanced on Solferino. One division, the 3rd (Mallard), was to start from Desenzano and explore the country between the road along the shores of the lake and the railway line; another, the 5th (Cuchiari), was to start from the slopes behind Desenzano, follow the railway line as far as its intersection by the road from Rivoltella to Pozzolengo, then turn up this latter road and march on Pozzolengo; a third division, the 1st (Durando) starting from the hills of Lonato, was to follow the ridge to Castel Venzago, Madonna della Scoperta, and on to Pozzolengo, where it was to unite with the column coming from the other side. It would be too long for a narrative of this kind to go into all the details of this struggle, which, however brilliant and brave, played only a subordinate part in deciding the fate of the day, and it will be sufficient to indicate its chief merits and its general character.

A look at the map will show that the Austrian general at Pozzolengo had all the advantages of position, being at Pozzolengo in the centre, and having the heights of San Martino and Madonna della Scoperta to his right and left front. The Sardinians, coming from Desenzano and Lonato, at an angle to these two positions in advance of Pozzolengo had to change their front to attack them, and by so doing, the column of San Martino exposed its right flank and line of retreat to Desenzano, and the column of Madonna della Scoperta its left flank. General Benedeck, from his central position at Pozzolengo, or rather on the long ridge in front of it, was on the right flank of one and on the left of the other; and whenever one or the other column carried the position, it was again forced to abandon it by a fresh Austrian column threatening to cut off its retreat. The ground, thickly covered as it is with trees, considerably improved these advantages of the Austrians by hiding their movements from the Piedmontese.

Another thing which made the task of the Piedmontese doubly difficult was, that their disposition and order of march was not calculated for an attack so much as for a reconnaissance; the consequence was that the troops, instead of making a combined effort from the beginning, had to continue these partial efforts in order to keep open their line of retreat, which was constantly threatened.

The first detachment sent as reconnaissance on the San Martino line consisted merely of a battalion of Bersaglieri, a battalion of infantry, two guns, and a squadron of *chevaux légers*, all belonging to the 5th division. It comes along the railway-line, passes San Martino—which was not occupied at the time—and turns up the road to Pozzolengo, finds the enemy in great force, and has to turn back. General Mallard, who hears the musketry, and the sound of guns, sends the vanguard of his division, the 3rd, and instead of following his line towards Peschiera, he comes just in time to take San Martino, and thus free the line of retreat for the first detachment; but already the Austrians have taken a position lower down on the railway, threatening thus to cut off this line of communication. In order to prevent this, the first brigade of the 3rd division, which just then arrives from Rivoltella at the railway line, is sent up against the heights, takes them twice, and has to turn back from the fresh reinforcements which the enemy has at hand. The line of the railway was thus in the hands of the Austrians, and the line of retreat of the Sardinian force thus again compromised. At ten a.m. the 5th division comes up; one brigade of it is sent on to the road to Pozzolengo to turn the right flank of the position, and all the rest of the troops present make a brilliant effort, and succeed in successively gaining all the positions, and losing them again successively just at the moment when the 2nd brigade of the 3rd division arrives and forms in line of battle. It was then about noon; the troops had been fighting under fearful disadvantages since the morning, and it was clearly necessary to wait for reinforcements. The 4th division of the Sardinian army being at Salo and in the mountains near Lake Idro, the 1st division engaged since the morning at Madonna della Scoperta, and obliged to fall back, no reserve remained except the 2nd division (Fanti). This was to have marched on Solferino to co-operate with the French; but, considering the emergency of the case, the 1st brigade of it was sent to support the 1st division in the direction of Madonna della Scoperta, and the 2nd (Aosta) sent to support the other two at San Martino. When this arrived, a general attack took place on both points. It was just after the last sounds of thunder had died away in the storm which swept over the battlefield, about half-past five to six p.m., and was decisive; eighteen guns were concentrated into one battery, to demolish the Cascina Contracagna, which had been the chief *appui* of the Austrians on their left, and all their positions were successfully taken by nightfall.[2]

Somewhat earlier than this attack on San Martino, the final attack on Madonna della Scoperta took place, which was less difficult than it might have been. Solferino was lost, and with the allies in Cavriana, Madonna della Scoperta was untenable. This column was therefore, after taking the latter place, advanced on Pozzolengo, and towards San Martino, and had several encounters with the rear-guard of the enemy, who was falling back on parallel lines. The road to Monzambano being taken up by the 5th Austrian corps, which had been pressed in that direction after the loss of Solferino, the 8th

---

2. Mr. Bossoli's two spirited sketches represent this final assault on both points; all the most prominent points are visible. San Martino in the centre, and the enemy grouped about it. In No. 37 the church of Madonna della Scoperta.

corps, which had fought at Pozzolengo, retired over the Mincio at Salionze, followed till late at night by the Sardinians.

What the fight was on the Sardinian side may be seen from their losses: 49 officers killed, 167 wounded; 642 men killed, 3,405 wounded; 1,258 dispersed and prisoners: so that next morning, at roll-call, the Sardinian army was short of 5,525 men. Some of the regiments and battalions had a fourth of their number *hors de combat*, one battalion of Bersaglieri had 7 officers killed or wounded out of 13. To set off against this were five guns which fell into the hands of the Sardinians, and the position of Pozzolengo.

The French losses were not less heavy: the 4th corps, which had had the fighting on the other wing, had 4,809 men, and of these 260 officers *hors de combat*; the 1st corps, 234 officers and above 4,000 men; the 2nd corps, 113 officers and 1,700 men. Strange enough, the *voltigeurs* and *chasseurs-à-pied* of the Garde, who decided the day, had no great losses; indeed, they were so small in comparison with what they did, that the official account says nothing of them; from what one saw, they had probably not a couple of hundred men killed and wounded. The 3rd corps had 15 officers and 200 men killed and wounded. So that the loss of the allies amounted to 16,000 or 17,000 men *hors de combat*. The trophies were, 30 guns, 3 stand of colours, and several thousand prisoners. The Austrian losses cannot have been less than the losses of the allies; for if one remembers that they had time enough to remove their wounded from Solferino during the hardest part of the fight, that they could do the same from Cavriana and Guidizzolo, and that they themselves acknowledge that their reserves were reached by the French rifled guns: this is the necessary conclusion from the number of dead and wounded they left on the battlefield.

But it was not the actual gain or loss in men and material which gave the Battle of Solferino its importance, nor was it even the gain by the allies and loss by the Austrians of the position on the Mincio hills, and the passage of that river. It was the moral effect naturally produced by a transition from exaggerated hopes and confidence to their very reverse. Twenty-four hours before, the Austrian soldier had seen the thousands and thousands of his comrades crossing the river, and he felt confident of success. He saw this confidence greatly exaggerated in his officers. He expects to carry everything before him—that is, at least, the promise of his superiors; and before he has time to shake sleep from his eyes, he sees an impetuous host rushing upon him, provided with more formidable weapons than his, having fresh troops and reserves where his side can count none. He has not time to eat a morsel before he must shoulder his musket, fight throughout a long summer day in the sun, and find himself, after many incidents and hair-breadth escapes, on the banks of the river which he had crossed so triumphantly the previous day. The thousands who yesterday crossed with all the military regularity in which the Austrian army excels, he now finds huddled together like a herd pursued by wolves, crowding over the bridge in almost hopeless confusion, and, wounded, exhausted, separated from his companions, he arrives at the left bank of the Mincio.

The victory was decisive; for the Austrian army which had fought at Solferino was demoralized, and unable to stand against the victors in open field. Ten times as many guns, and five times as many prisoners as the allies took would have been nothing in comparison to this result, which certainly the battle of Solferino obtained.

How this came to pass may have appeared from the narrative of events, and the remarks which were thought necessary to show these events in their true light: still, it is not until all the phases of an event are known, that it can be duly appreciated and understood; it will be, therefore, not out of place to say a few words to help this appreciation.

The return of the Austrians across the Mincio has been, as failures usually are, differently judged; some seeing in it only a rashness and folly, others a laudable boldness. The Austrians had ten *corps d'armée*, or over 200,000 men, concentrated between Verona and Mantua. They had the two fortresses of Mantua and Peschiera, and four other passages between the two—they could therefore throw across as many bridges as they chose. The allies had only occupied the outskirts of the Mincio hills, and they were not more than 130,000 to 140,000 strong. If the allies occupied the centre of the Mincio hills the river could no longer be defended; if the Austrians delayed their attack, the two strong divisions of Prince Napoleon would have come up, and 18,000 or 20,000 men have been added to the allied armies. All this was ground enough for an offensive movement. There were, however, two considerations which should not have been overlooked: first, whether there was time to take up a position before the allies could attack; secondly, whether the troops had sufficiently recovered from the effects, physical and moral, which the inauspicious opening of the campaign must have had upon them. The first point was successfully proved by the Austrians themselves, who with admirable skill threw nine *corps d'armée* across the Mincio in one day, without baggage, it is true, but still not without a waggon-train. The event of the battle decided the second question against the Austrians. Solferino, San Cassiano, and Cavriana, three as formidable positions in their *ensemble* as are ever to met with, were defended by three Austrian corps, in all at least 60,000 men, and were attacked and taken by three French corps, in all certainly not more than 50,000 men. There was very little skill to be displayed on either side—the only thing to be done was to fight as resolutely as possible. That the Austrian officers did not foresee such a result, or even suspect it, is caused by the little communication they have with, and the little they know of their soldier; they supposed in him the same *esprit de corps* and desire to wipe out the blot of Magenta as they themselves felt.

As for the movement by which they hoped to do this, it shows an amusing disregard of the simplest rules of strategy; they wanted to turn the flank of the enemy and cut him off from his line of retreat, and chose the longest and most difficult lines of operation. The line of operations of the allies was centred in Brescia, and from this centre two roads lead to the Mincio, one by Lonato in an almost straight line intersecting the Mincio at right angles at Peschiera; the other diverging from Brescia in a south-easterly direction, at a considerable angle from the first, and running through Castiglione to Goito. These two lines, with that of the Mincio, form a rectangular triangle, the Mincio forming the base, Peschiera the right angle, and Brescia the apex. Now, it is not necessary to be a great commander to know that the shortest road from the base of a rectangular triangle to its apex is from the rectangle. Whatever be the opinion entertained of Austrian generals after the Italian campaign of 1859, it can scarcely be supposed they were ignorant of this geometrical simple

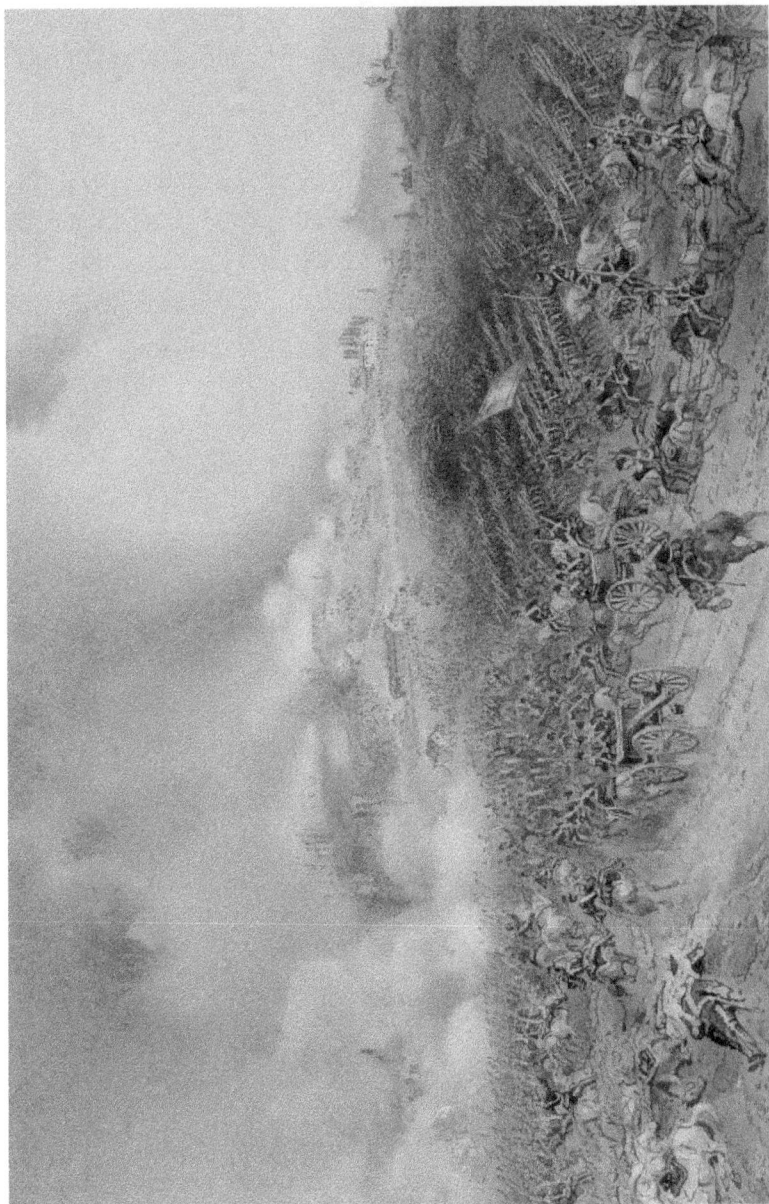

BATTLE OF SOLFERINO—ATTACK OF S. MARTINA BY THE PIEDMONTESE

truth, especially as the dispositions of the allies were such, as to force it upon them. On this shortest line, there was only the Sardinian army before them, which, having sent off one of its divisions to the mountains, was not more than 25,000 fighting men. The Austrians could not be ignorant of this fact in a country where the priesthood and most of the peasantry is, or at any rate was, for them—they had Peschiera and two other passages over the Mincio. If, instead of sending off three whole corps in the wrong direction, they had only sent, on their natural line of operations, two or even one of them, which they might have done without taking off one man from their position, the Sardinian army could not have resisted, overpowered as it would have been by numbers, and the Austrian flanking columns would have been in Lonato, in the rear of the French army, probably long before the French had a chance of taking Solferino. The fear of being thrown into the lake could not influence them, for there would have been less danger of this contingency for two or three corps than there was for one.

If, therefore, in spite of all reasons which seemed to prescribe an effort on the side towards the lake, this effort was made in the plain, we cannot but think that the Austrians chose that side because they expected the success would be more complete; for instance—taking half the army prisoners, and driving the other half into the Chiese.

The same strange confidence in success seems to have prevailed up to the last moment; no one could otherwise explain how the Austrians could extend their position in advance of Solferino for several miles, and try to resist at Grole, almost two miles from Solferino, instead of concentrating their forces where the real effort was to be made. Their confidence was probably increased by that greatest of fallacies, the successive positions which extended up to Solferino; as if soldiers would ever exert themselves to hold a good position in front, knowing there is a still better one in the rear; and as if they could ever be reckoned upon to hold a position in the rear, after having been driven back from one or two in front.

Besides this strange confidence in success, which we meet everywhere, there is another inference which is unavoidable, and this is, that the emperor Francis Joseph's taking the command did not improve the direction of affairs, for there was everywhere the same kind of Bashi-Bazuk style as there had been under General Gyulai at Magenta—corps advancing or retiring just as it suited them, appearing or not appearing; in fact, every one for himself and no one for all.

There never was anything more true than the saying that in warfare he has invariably the best of it who makes the fewest blunders. It was difficult to make more than the Austrians; but the Emperor Napoleon did not lose the opportunity of profiting by these blunders. If Austrian generalship was much the same at Solferino as at Magenta, although the general had been changed, we see in the command of the allied army, on the contrary, a great difference, although the commander was the same. At Magenta, it was the first *début*, with unavoidable mistakes; at Solferino the imperial *débutant* shows himself master of his art. There is not a battle in which there are not some improvements which suggest themselves *after the event*, and no doubt Solferino forms no exception; but there rarely was a battle with fewer false moves than Solferino.

For the over-caution of Marshal Canrobert, if there really was over-caution, the commander-in-chief can scarcely be made responsible; for, having to remain on the point where the decisive blow was struck, he had to leave it to the judgment of the commanders on the right wing whether there seemed a chance of the Austrian flanking column coming up or not, and how far it was safe to weaken the corps which had to keep it in check.

It will be remembered that there was an angry correspondence on the subject between the two generals commanding the 4th and 3rd corps; the event proved Marshal Niel to be in the right, for though during the whole day clouds of dust were seen, no flanking columns showed themselves. No doubt the probability was, that one at least of three *corps d'armée* might find its way in that direction, and it seemed almost folly to weaken the 3rd corps. The emperor had chosen Canrobert for the defence of the right wing during the advance, because he knew he could trust his prudence. But after the taking of the heights of Solferino, and the advance of the 2nd corps, that this prudence might have been much more relaxed than it was, was the general opinion in the French army, the gallant marshal's own corps not excepted, which, as is well known, was nicknamed by its comrades *la providence des familles*.

CHAPTER 10

The Passage of the Mincio

At seven p.m. the order arrived at Castiglione to transfer headquarters to Cavriana the same evening. Most of the corps bivouacked on the spot which they had occupied last; the Garde Impérials and the second corps at Cavriana, the fourth corps on the spot where it had fought the whole day, the third corps where it had been waiting for the flanking-column, and the first corps in the direction of Pozzolengo; so that the left wing and the centre of the allies was again in contact. Only the division Bazaine of this corps followed the Austrians for some time; but it fell back, and the Austrians were not at all disturbed in their retreat.

Next morning, the first corps occupies Pozzolengo, the Sardinians draw towards Ponte and to the neighbourhood of Peschiera; the rest of the allied armies remain on the ground which they had occupied before, busy with picking up the wounded and burying the dead. When the armies arrived at Brescia, measures were taken to prepare 6,000 beds. The French alone had almost double that number of wounded. Besides, Brescia is about fifteen miles from Castiglione, and this latter place itself above five miles from some of the places where the fight had gone on. All the carts and carriages which could be got were put in requisition to remove the wounded from the battlefield, and take them to Castiglione. In this latter place, houses, churches, streets, barns, courtyards, were all one great hospital; there was scarcely a room in which there were not one or two wounded, friend and foe. The first moments after battles are always full of confusion, but very few places ever came up probably in this respect to Castiglione, as it was in the evening of the 24th, when the long processions of wounded were coming in, and the baggage of head-quarters and of the whole Imperial Guard trying to get out by the same road; every one trying to find his own, and get it through the crowd; begging, cursing, threatening, ordering, joking,—in fact, resorting to every imaginable means to gain a few steps towards the entrance of the village. All those coming in from the battlefield were running wild about in search of food and drink. Reserve ammunition, which was not wanted, blocking the road in one direction; baggage-carts, which were very much wanted, not able to pass in another direction; wounded waiting in the streets because there was no possibility of making room for their passage; the soldiers belonging to the ambulances calling out for room in one direction, a forlorn *gendarme* in another, an officer in a third direction. One might almost have imagined oneself in a crowd after a defeat, had it not been for the good humour which prevailed, and the care which was taken of the wounded. By dawn, the greater part of the baggage had left Castiglione, and then things became a little more orderly, and the wounded were henceforth the objects of all care; and they certainly required it, for every moment new mule and cartloads of them were brought to Castiglione. The procession seemed endless, and in the beginning it appeared almost hopeless to bring them under cover. Everything was full, and numbers had to be laid along the sides of the houses until those who could bear transporting to Brescia could be forwarded in that direction. And these were only the wounded from Solferino and the right; those from S. Martino went to Desenzano, and were sent by Lonato to Brescia.

Here likewise nothing like the accommodation required could be found, and it was equally necessary to call in the assistance of the inhabitants; and certainly Brescia may be proud of its population, for nothing could be more striking than its noble and patriotic conduct. Not a house or family, however small, which did not find means to accommodate one or more of the wounded, and many deprived themselves not only of their comforts, but of necessaries, in order to relieve the sufferings of those who fought for them. All those who had carriages at their disposal went out themselves to the French and Piedmontese lines, to bring back wounded. Others

Interview of the emperors of France and Austria at Villafranca

were waiting at the gates of the town for their arrival, and carried off the wounded as if they were a treasure which they had found; others again, in order to be beforehand in the work of patriotism and charity, went several miles on the road to meet and invite them to their abodes.

All these efforts made to alleviate the sufferings of the wounded were suddenly disturbed on the 25th by one of those panics which are common the day after a battle, when the excitement has not had time to abate, and all minds are still very sensitive to any outward impression. It came from the Campo di Medole, but its real cause has never been quite ascertained. The 2nd French hussars, whose uniform in the distance might be taken for Austrians, got the credit of it in the army, although there were several rather suspicious-looking Chasseurs d'Afrique remarked by many people. Already on the day of the battle they excited indignation by the way in which they galloped at full speed among the ambulances, and one of these identical chasseurs was the first to spread the rumour in Castiglione.

But however this be, at three p.m. a column of dust rose on the highroad from the Campo di Medole to Castiglione, and veiled by this white cover was a rush of mules, carts, and carriages, coursing along as hard as they could, jolting the wounded, throwing them to the right and left, upsetting and breaking everything. Before the rush reached Castiglione the confusion had spread there. The sick who could still walk tried to get off; it was a general *sauve qui peut*; officers, men, sick and sound, *gendarmes*, infantry, cavalry, artillery, train; in one word, every one made off. With incredible rapidity, almost by telegraph it seemed, the rumour that the Austrians were back spread even to Brescia, causing no slight alarm. However, in an hour the whole was over; but it cost the life of many a poor fellow, and heavy punishment to more than one officer.

In the mean time the Austrians had quietly retired on the 25th, and burned down the wooden bridges at Monzambano, Valeggio, and Goito, where they were still standing. It was only slowly that the allied army took up its position on the Mincio. This delay was at the time attributed to the necessity of giving the siege-train the necessary time to arrive, and to the wish of effecting a junction with the 5th corps (Prince Napoleon), which was coming up from

Tuscany. One division of it (d'Antemarre) was already at Pradura on the Oglio, but the other part was still on the right bank of the Po, over which a bridge was constructed at Casal Maggiore on the 28th. By that time the allied armies were occupying a line in the Mincio hills from Peschiera to Monzambano, Borghetto, Volta, down towards Goito. The Sardinians, who kept the left wing, had gradually drawn nearer to Peschiera, investing it from the lake to the right bank of the Mincio. To the right was the 1st French corps which had advanced from Pozzolengo to Ponti and Salionze; on its right the 2nd, which had come from Cavriana, and which had its direction on Monzambano. Further, the 4th had gone to Volta, and was preparing to cross at Borghetto; the 3rd, forming the extreme right, was watching Goito. On the 29th, the bridges being ready at Ponti, Monzambano, and Borghetto, a simultaneous advance was made, and the 4th corps pushed its vanguard to Villafranca, the others taking their position on the little river Tione which comes out of the Mincio hills on the left bank of the river. The Imperial Guard the same day followed the emperor to Volta, which became the general headquarters.

As the Sardinians drew nearer to Peschiera the fortress opened its fire upon them. The investment of Peschiera on the west and south side, took place in the night of the 29th-30th, and early in the morning the first shots were already heard succeeding each other rapidly. And from that day it continued until the armistice was concluded. The fire usually began early in the morning, ceased in the forenoon, and began again towards evening.

On the 1st of July the imperial headquarters were transferred to Valeggio, on the left bank of the Mincio, and those of the king from Rivoltella to Monzambano. The events from this moment are related in very few words. The Sardinians close in upon Peschiera; they open their trenches on the night of the 2nd, but never get their guns up. The 1st French corps pushes forward to Castelnuovo, the centre of the roads between Peschiera, Verona, Mantua, and the valley of the Adige, and occupies Piacenza on the Lago di Garda, thus making the investment of Peschiera from the land-side complete. In the meantime the siege-train is beginning to arrive. On the 1st of July the railway communication between Genoa and Desenzano on the Lago di Garda is complete. Not only have all the bridges been repaired, but also the breaks which have hitherto existed in the line. The line in its whole course is inaugurated by the gunboats, which had been ready for some time and waiting at Casale for the completion of the railway line. As soon as they arrive they are put together, and when the Peace of Villafranca is signed on the 12th, five of them are almost completed. The 5th corps, which has at last effected its passage, comes up and takes a position in second line at Salionze between the 1st at Castelnuovo and the 2nd at Oliosi. The 3rd corps had likewise passed on pontoon bridges a little below Valeggio at Pozzolo. Thus, by the 2nd, the whole French army was on the left bank of the Mincio, occupying a curved line from the shores of the lake by Castelnuovo along the Tione into the plain, and from thence down to Valeggio and Pozzolo.

Everyone was speculating on the movements of the Austrians, who were known to have withdrawn to the neighbourhood of Verona and Mantua, or else indulging in conjectures about the arrival of the siege train, or trying to make the best of the terrific heat and the crowded camp, when, on the 3rd, the arrival of a son of General Urban, as *parlementaire*, gave a different direction to all thoughts, and created rumours of an armistice and hopes of peace. The *parlementaire* came with an autograph letter, in which the Emperor Francis Joseph thanked the Emperor Napoleon for sending back some wounded officers, who had been taken at Guidizzolo. This letter, it seems, became the starting-point for the negotiation. It was supposed that the parlementaire sent by the Piedmontese to negotiate the exchange of the prisoners of Palestro against those of San Martin o was the first overture. This is strongly denied by the Piedmontese; at any rate, on the evening of the 6th, General Fleury, accompanied by his *aide-de-camp* leaves Valeggio for Verona; he arrives there in the night at ten p.m.; he has an audience of the emperor of Austria, and an interview with Count Rechberg and returns next morning at nine with the news of the armistice. The same morning the whole French army was under arms at three a.m., and made a grand military promenade in advance, but was back again by seven a.m.

Next day, the 8th, the chiefs of the staff of the two armies had a meeting at Villafranca, to arrange the conditions of the armistice.

It was fixed from the next day to the 10th of August; the basis of it was the *status quo* of occupation, with a neutral ground between the two armies.

From this moment there is a constant communication between the commanders of the two armies, which ends in the interview of Villafranca,—and peace.

The Emperor Napoleon, accompanied by Marshal Vaillant, Generals Martimprey and Fleury, his military household, and the Cent-Gardes, started at nine a.m. from Valeggio; while the Emperor Francis Joseph, accompanied by a brilliant staff, the *gendarmerie* of the guard, and two squadrons of lancers, left Verona at ten a.m. for Villafranca. The Emperor Napoleon was the first to arrive at the spot, and finding that his imperial brother was only a short distance off, he went to meet him on the road. When the two emperors approached each other, their respective escorts fell back, leaving them in front. The Emperor Napoleon took off his *kepi*, and shook hands with the emperor of Austria, after which both turned back towards Villafranca.

At Villafranca the house of M. Carlo Gaudini Morelli had been prepared to receive the two sovereigns. It was the same in which the emperor of Austria had passed the night before the Battle of Solferino. The two emperors entered, and a French *cent-garde* and an Austrian *gendarme* were placed as sentries before the door. After an hour or so the interview was over, and the two emperors came out. They presented to each other their respective staffs, and then mounted again on horseback, the Emperor Francis Joseph accompanying the emperor of the French for some distance on the road to Valeggio, after which there was an exchange of cordialities, and each went his own way.

The same night the Treaty of Peace was signed, and the next day the army took up the position which it was to occupy until it was withdrawn. The Imperial Guard arrived at Desenzano, whither the emperor also transferred his headquarters on the 13th; on the 14th he made his second entry into Milan; and two days after he was back in France, after an absence of two months and a few days, having won two great battles, humiliated Austria, given Lombardy to Piedmont, acquired the greatest military renown in his generation, supreme ascendancy in Italian affairs, and in the eyes of his own people and of Europe.

LEONAUR

ALSO FROM LEONAUR
AVAILABLE IN SOFTCOVER OR HARDCOVER WITH DUST JACKET

AT THEM WITH THE BAYONET *by Donald F. Featherstone*—The first Anglo-Sikh War 1845-1846.

STEPHEN CRANE'S BATTLES *by Stephen Crane*—Nine Decisive Battles Recounted by the Author of 'The Red Badge of Courage'.

THE GURKHA WAR *by H. T. Prinsep*—The Anglo-Nepalese Conflict in North East India 1814-1816.

FIRE & BLOOD *by G. R. Gleig*—The burning of Washington & the battle of New Orleans, 1814, through the eyes of a young British soldier.

SOUND ADVANCE! *by Joseph Anderson*—Experiences of an officer of HM 50th regiment in Australia, Burma & the Gwalior war.

THE CAMPAIGN OF THE INDUS *by Thomas Holdsworth*—Experiences of a British Officer of the 2nd (Queen's Royal) Regiment in the Campaign to Place Shah Shuja on the Throne of Afghanistan 1838 - 1840.

WITH THE MADRAS EUROPEAN REGIMENT IN BURMA *by John Butler*—The Experiences of an Officer of the Honourable East India Company's Army During the First Anglo-Burmese War 1824 - 1826.

IN ZULULAND WITH THE BRITISH ARMY *by Charles L. Norris-Newman*—The Anglo-Zulu war of 1879 through the first-hand experiences of a special correspondent.

BESIEGED IN LUCKNOW *by Martin Richard Gubbins*—The first Anglo-Sikh War 1845-1846.

A TIGER ON HORSEBACK *by L. March Phillips*—The Experiences of a Trooper & Officer of Rimington's Guides - The Tigers - during the Anglo-Boer war 1899 - 1902.

SEPOYS, SIEGE & STORM *by Charles John Griffiths*—The Experiences of a young officer of H.M.'s 61st Regiment at Ferozepore, Delhi ridge and at the fall of Delhi during the Indian mutiny 1857.

CAMPAIGNING IN ZULULAND *by W. E. Montague*—Experiences on campaign during the Zulu war of 1879 with the 94th Regiment.

THE STORY OF THE GUIDES *by G.J. Younghusband*—The Exploits of the Soldiers of the famous Indian Army Regiment from the northwest frontier 1847 - 1900.

LEONAUR

ALSO FROM LEONAUR
AVAILABLE IN SOFTCOVER OR HARDCOVER WITH DUST JACKET

ZULU:1879 *by D.C.F. Moodie & the Leonaur Editors*—The Anglo-Zulu War of 1879 from contemporary sources: First Hand Accounts, Interviews, Dispatches, Official Documents & Newspaper Reports.

THE RED DRAGOON *by W.J. Adams*—With the 7th Dragoon Guards in the Cape of Good Hope against the Boers & the Kaffir tribes during the 'war of the axe' 1843-48'.

THE RECOLLECTIONS OF SKINNER OF SKINNER'S HORSE *by James Skinner*—James Skinner and his 'Yellow Boys' Irregular cavalry in the wars of India between the British, Mahratta, Rajput, Mogul, Sikh & Pindarree Forces.

A CAVALRY OFFICER DURING THE SEPOY REVOLT *by A. R. D. Mackenzie*—Experiences with the 3rd Bengal Light Cavalry, the Guides and Sikh Irregular Cavalry from the outbreak to Delhi and Lucknow.

A NORFOLK SOLDIER IN THE FIRST SIKH WAR *by J W Baldwin*—Experiences of a private of H.M. 9th Regiment of Foot in the battles for the Punjab, India 1845-6.

TOMMY ATKINS' WAR STORIES: 14 FIRST HAND ACCOUNTS—Fourteen first hand accounts from the ranks of the British Army during Queen Victoria's Empire.

THE WATERLOO LETTERS *by H. T. Siborne*—Accounts of the Battle by British Officers for its Foremost Historian.

NEY: GENERAL OF CAVALRY VOLUME 1—1769-1799 *by Antoine Bulos*—The Early Career of a Marshal of the First Empire.

NEY: MARSHAL OF FRANCE VOLUME 2—1799-1805 *by Antoine Bulos*—The Early Career of a Marshal of the First Empire.

AIDE-DE-CAMP TO NAPOLEON *by Philippe-Paul de Ségur*—For anyone interested in the Napoleonic Wars this book, written by one who was intimate with the strategies and machinations of the Emperor, will be essential reading.

TWILIGHT OF EMPIRE *by Sir Thomas Ussher & Sir George Cockburn*—Two accounts of Napoleon's Journeys in Exile to Elba and St. Helena: Narrative of Events by Sir Thomas Ussher & Napoleon's Last Voyage: Extract of a diary by Sir George Cockburn.

PRIVATE WHEELER *by William Wheeler*—The letters of a soldier of the 51st Light Infantry during the Peninsular War & at Waterloo.

ALSO FROM LEONAUR

AVAILABLE IN SOFTCOVER OR HARDCOVER WITH DUST JACKET

OFFICERS & GENTLEMEN *by Peter Hawker & William Graham*—Two Accounts of British Officers During the Peninsula War: Officer of Light Dragoons by Peter Hawker & Campaign in Portugal and Spain by William Graham .

THE WALCHEREN EXPEDITION *by Anonymous*—The Experiences of a British Officer of the 81st Regt. During the Campaign in the Low Countries of 1809.

LADIES OF WATERLOO *by Charlotte A. Eaton, Magdalene de Lancey & Juana Smith*—The Experiences of Three Women During the Campaign of 1815: Waterloo Days by Charlotte A. Eaton, A Week at Waterloo by Magdalene de Lancey & Juana's Story by Juana Smith.

JOURNAL OF AN OFFICER IN THE KING'S GERMAN LEGION *by John Frederick Hering*—Recollections of Campaigning During the Napoleonic Wars.

JOURNAL OF AN ARMY SURGEON IN THE PENINSULAR WAR *by Charles Boutflower*—The Recollections of a British Army Medical Man on Campaign During the Napoleonic Wars.

ON CAMPAIGN WITH MOORE AND WELLINGTON *by Anthony Hamilton*—The Experiences of a Soldier of the 43rd Regiment During the Peninsular War.

THE ROAD TO AUSTERLITZ *by R. G. Burton*—Napoleon's Campaign of 1805.

SOLDIERS OF NAPOLEON *by A. J. Doisy De Villargennes & Arthur Chuquet*—The Experiences of the Men of the French First Empire: Under the Eagles by A. J. Doisy De Villargennes & Voices of 1812 by Arthur Chuquet .

INVASION OF FRANCE, 1814 *by F. W. O. Maycock*—The Final Battles of the Napoleonic First Empire.

LEIPZIG—A CONFLICT OF TITANS *by Frederic Shoberl*—A Personal Experience of the 'Battle of the Nations' During the Napoleonic Wars, October 14th-19th, 1813.

SLASHERS *by Charles Cadell*—The Campaigns of the 28th Regiment of Foot During the Napoleonic Wars by a Serving Officer.

BATTLE IMPERIAL *by Charles William Vane*—The Campaigns in Germany & France for the Defeat of Napoleon 1813-1814.

SWIFT & BOLD *by Gibbes Rigaud*—The 60th Rifles During the Peninsula War.

LEONAUR

ALSO FROM LEONAUR
AVAILABLE IN SOFTCOVER OR HARDCOVER WITH DUST JACKET

LEONAUR

ALSO FROM LEONAUR
AVAILABLE IN SOFTCOVER OR HARDCOVER WITH DUST JACKET

CAPTAIN COIGNET *by Jean-Roch Coignet*—A Soldier of Napoleon's Imperial Guard from the Italian Campaign to Russia and Waterloo.

HUSSAR ROCCA *by Albert Jean Michel de Rocca*—A French cavalry officer's experiences of the Napoleonic Wars and his views on the Peninsular Campaigns against the Spanish, British And Guerilla Armies.

MARINES TO 95TH (RIFLES) *by Thomas Fernyhough*—The military experiences of Robert Fernyhough during the Napoleonic Wars.

LIGHT BOB *by Robert Blakeney*—The experiences of a young officer in H.M 28th & 36th regiments of the British Infantry during the Peninsular Campaign of the Napoleonic Wars 1804 - 1814.

WITH WELLINGTON'S LIGHT CAVALRY *by William Tomkinson*—The Experiences of an officer of the 16th Light Dragoons in the Peninsular and Waterloo campaigns of the Napoleonic Wars.

SERGEANT BOURGOGNE *by Adrien Bourgogne*—With Napoleon's Imperial Guard in the Russian Campaign and on the Retreat from Moscow 1812 - 13.

SURTEES OF THE 95TH (RIFLES) *by William Surtees*—A Soldier of the 95th (Rifles) in the Peninsular campaign of the Napoleonic Wars.

SWORDS OF HONOUR *by Henry Newbolt & Stanley L. Wood*—The Careers of Six Outstanding Officers from the Napoleonic Wars, the Wars for India and the American Civil War.

ENSIGN BELL IN THE PENINSULAR WAR *by George Bell*—The Experiences of a young British Soldier of the 34th Regiment 'The Cumberland Gentlemen' in the Napoleonic wars.

HUSSAR IN WINTER *by Alexander Gordon*—A British Cavalry Officer during the retreat to Corunna in the Peninsular campaign of the Napoleonic Wars.

THE COMPLEAT RIFLEMAN HARRIS *by Benjamin Harris as told to and transcribed by Captain Henry Curling, 52nd Regt. of Foot*—The adventures of a soldier of the 95th (Rifles) during the Peninsular Campaign of the Napoleonic Wars.

THE ADVENTURES OF A LIGHT DRAGOON *by George Farmer & G.R. Gleig*—A cavalryman during the Peninsular & Waterloo Campaigns, in captivity & at the siege of Bhurtpore, India.

LEONAUR

ALSO FROM LEONAUR
AVAILABLE IN SOFTCOVER OR HARDCOVER WITH DUST JACKET

LIFE IN THE ARMY OF NORTHERN VIRGINIA *by Carlton McCarthy—* The Observations of a Confederate Artilleryman of Cutshaw's Battalion During the American Civil War 1861-1865.

HISTORY OF THE CAVALRY OF THE ARMY OF THE POTOMAC *by Charles D. Rhodes—*Including Pope's Army of Virginia and the Cavalry Operations in West Virginia During the American Civil War.

CAMP-FIRE AND COTTON-FIELD *by Thomas W. Knox—*A New York Herald Correspondent's View of the American Civil War.

SERGEANT STILLWELL *by Leander Stillwell* —The Experiences of a Union Army Soldier of the 61st Illinois Infantry During the American Civil War.

STONEWALL'S CANNONEER *by Edward A. Moore—*Experiences with the Rockbridge Artillery, Confederate Army of Northern Virginia, During the American Civil War.

THE SIXTH CORPS *by George Stevens—*The Army of the Potomac, Union Army, During the American Civil War.

THE RAILROAD RAIDERS *by William Pittenger—*An Ohio Volunteers Recollections of the Andrews Raid to Disrupt the Confederate Railroad in Georgia During the American Civil War.

CITIZEN SOLDIER *by John Beatty—*An Account of the American Civil War by a Union Infantry Officer of Ohio Volunteers Who Became a Brigadier General.

COX: PERSONAL RECOLLECTIONS OF THE CIVIL WAR--VOLUME 1 *by Jacob Dolson Cox—*West Virginia, Kanawha Valley, Gauley Bridge, Cotton Mountain, South Mountain, Antietam, the Morgan Raid & the East Tennessee Campaign.

COX: PERSONAL RECOLLECTIONS OF THE CIVIL WAR--VOLUME 2 *by Jacob Dolson Cox—*Siege of Knoxville, East Tennessee, Atlanta Campaign, the Nashville Campaign & the North Carolina Campaign.

KERSHAW'S BRIGADE VOLUME 1 *by D. Augustus Dickert—*Manassas, Seven Pines, Sharpsburg (Antietam), Fredricksburg, Chancellorsville, Gettysburg, Chickamauga, Chattanooga, Fort Sanders & Bean Station.

KERSHAW'S BRIGADE VOLUME 2 *by D. Augustus Dickert—*At the wilderness, Cold Harbour, Petersburg, The Shenandoah Valley and Cedar Creek..

LEONAUR

ALSO FROM LEONAUR
AVAILABLE IN SOFTCOVER OR HARDCOVER WITH DUST JACKET

ESCAPE FROM THE FRENCH *by Edward Boys*—A Young Royal Navy Midshipman's Adventures During the Napoleonic War.

THE VOYAGE OF H.M.S. PANDORA *by Edward Edwards R. N. & George Hamilton, edited by Basil Thomson*—In Pursuit of the Mutineers of the Bounty in the South Seas—1790-1791.

MEDUSA *by J. B. Henry Savigny and Alexander Correard and Charlotte-Adélaïde Dard* —Narrative of a Voyage to Senegal in 1816 & The Sufferings of the Picard Family After the Shipwreck of the Medusa.

THE SEA WAR OF 1812 VOLUME 1 *by A. T. Mahan*—A History of the Maritime Conflict.

THE SEA WAR OF 1812 VOLUME 2 *by A. T. Mahan*—A History of the Maritime Conflict.

WETHERELL OF H. M. S. HUSSAR *by John Wetherell*—The Recollections of an Ordinary Seaman of the Royal Navy During the Napoleonic Wars.

THE NAVAL BRIGADE IN NATAL *by C. R. N. Burne*—With the Guns of H. M. S. Terrible & H. M. S. Tartar during the Boer War 1899-1900.

THE VOYAGE OF H. M. S. BOUNTY *by William Bligh*—The True Story of an 18th Century Voyage of Exploration and Mutiny.

SHIPWRECK! *by William Gilly*—The Royal Navy's Disasters at Sea 1793-1849.

KING'S CUTTERS AND SMUGGLERS: 1700-1855 *by E. Keble Chatterton*—A unique period of maritime history-from the beginning of the eighteenth to the middle of the nineteenth century when British seamen risked all to smuggle valuable goods from wool to tea and spirits from and to the Continent.

CONFEDERATE BLOCKADE RUNNER *by John Wilkinson*—The Personal Recollections of an Officer of the Confederate Navy.

NAVAL BATTLES OF THE NAPOLEONIC WARS *by W. H. Fitchett*—Cape St. Vincent, the Nile, Cadiz, Copenhagen, Trafalgar & Others.

PRISONERS OF THE RED DESERT *by R. S. Gwatkin-Williams*—The Adventures of the Crew of the Tara During the First World War.

U-BOAT WAR 1914-1918 *by James B. Connolly/Karl von Schenk*—Two Contrasting Accounts from Both Sides of the Conflict at Sea D uring the Great War.